WINNING FANTASY FOOTBALL

JUN - 2006

WINNING FANTASY FOOTBALL

How to Play and Win Your Fantasy Football League Every Year

STEPHEN NOVER

Cardoza Publishing

Cardoza Publishing is the foremost gaming publisher in the world, with a library of over 175 up-to-date and easy-to-read books and strategies. These authoritative works are written by the top experts in their fields and with more than 8,500,000 books in print, represent the best-selling and most popular gaming books anywhere.

FIRST EDITION

Copyright © 2005 by Stephen Nover
- All Rights Reserved -

Library of Congress Catalog Card No: 2005921679
ISBN: 1-58042-180-6

Visit our web site —www.cardozapub.com)—or write for a full list of books and computer strategies.

CARDOZA PUBLISHING
P.O. Box 1500, Cooper Station, New York, NY 10276
Phone (800) 577-WINS
email: cardozapub@aol.com
www.cardozapub.com

ABOUT THE AUTHOR

Stephen Nover is a multiple-award-winning writer and one of America's foremost fantasy football experts. Based in Las Vegas since 1984, Stephen has covered sports gaming and written fantasy football columns for a number of publications and Web sites, including the *Las Vegas Review-Journal, Insider's Football News, ATS Consultant's Fantasy Football Annual,* VegasInsider.com, and Covers.com, the largest online publisher of sports gaming in North America.

Stephen has finished in the money ten of eleven years in his Las Vegas Rotisserie-style football draft league, placing first five times. He has finished either first or second in his Las Vegas football auction league during the three years it's been held, and has also won numerous head-to-head format fantasy football leagues in ESPN and Yahoo leagues.

A 1977 graduate of the University of Wisconsin-Oshkosh, Stephen has worked for newspapers in Wisconsin, Iowa, Louisiana, and Nevada. He is the author of *Las Vegas Sports Beat* and *Sports Gaming Beat.*

TABLE OF CONTENTS

1. INTRODUCTION

Fantasy football is the greatest thing that has happened to the pro football fan in the last ten years. It's tremendous fun and a source of great pride to put together your own hand-picked team and "coach" them all the way to the championship. But there hasn't really been a book that teaches you how to play the game and shows you the strategies you need to win. Until now.

Fifteen chapters teach you everything you need to know to play and win at fantasy football—and not just this season but every year! From the basic rules of play—how to score points, draft players, and join existing leagues or start your own—to the insider strategies and the essential fundamentals of building a winning team, it's all here. You'll learn when to draft star players, how to get value deep down in the rounds, the tricks to finding sleepers and avoiding busts, how to improve your team through trades, pickups, and the waiver wire, and so much more.

You'll learn about the different leagues available—Head-to-Head, Rotisserie, Salary Cap and Keeper—and how to navigate your way around each of these formats, plus position by position and round by round strategies for both drafts and auctions.

You'll also learn how to play for free, or if you want to go for big prize money, sometimes over $100,000, you'll find out how to play those leagues as well.

It's a blast playing general manager and coach and choosing your team, setting your lineup, making trades, and picking up free agents. Imagine coaching Randy Moss, Ricky Williams, and Terrell Owens without the personal baggage that goes with them. Now you don't have to second-guess real coaches so much, because you're too busy pointing the finger at yourself. Hopefully it's not the wrong finger. Reading box scores will become exciting instead of just mundane. You never know when you might find a hidden gem such as your tight end getting 100 receiving yards in a game, or your kicker making a 50-yard field goal.

No longer will you just mainly be interested in your home team. Now you'll be involved with all thirty-two NFL teams. You'll have new players to root for and become more sophisticated in your knowledge of the league. You will become a lot sharper, especially about personnel, because you need to stay on top of the players. You will be able to spout off statistics faster than the coach—and not just the starters, either. You will have an idea about backups, team's defenses, and kickers.

No matter how lopsided the score of a real NFL game might be, you will still be involved. Every play has meaning. At any time, you could be picking up fantasy points, so you won't dare flip that television dial. One of the loudest screams I ever heard came at the end of a 34-0 game when a defender ran back a meaningless interception for a touchdown. Six more fantasy points just went on the board.

There's lots to talk about. Let's get started!

2. OVERVIEW

I started doing fantasy sports in the early 1990s. Back then some people considered you a geek or social misfit for participating in such an activity. It was estimated that fewer than one million people played fantasy football at that time. Now you're almost a social outcast if you aren't in a fantasy league. Fantasy football has made the hobby mainstream with an estimated fifteen million people involved. A 2004 *Sports Illustrated* poll found that 92 percent of fantasy participants compete in fantasy football.

I certainly wouldn't apply the term geek to Dan Marino, Curt Schilling, Bryant Gumbel, San Antonio Spurs guard Tony Parker, actor Michael J. Fox, singer Meat Loaf, and former governor of New York Mario Cuomo. They are all avid fantasy players. Jennie Finch, star pitcher and cover girl of the 2004 USA Olympic softball team, has a fantasy team, too. Still looking for a reason to play?

You could make a case that playing fantasy football is the number one fall and winter activity. It's actually scary how much men think about it. An online survey of men age twenty-two and over, conducted by

FantasyFootballChamps.com, found 40 percent saying fantasy football was their number one thought during the day. This compared to 30 percent who voted sex as their top thought. In this same survey, 25 percent responded that they spend four to eight hours each day thinking about fantasy football, while another 58 percent said they spend one to three hours per day.

One thing that has made football the most popular fantasy sports hobby is there are no complicated categories to be concerned about. In Rotisserie baseball, for instance, you have pitcher's ratio or WHIP. You don't need an advanced degree in calculus to add up touchdowns, passing yards, rushing yards, receiving yards, kicking points, sacks, fumbles, and interceptions. If you have all ten of your fingers, you're in good counting shape.

Internet Makes it Easy

The Internet has made the huge popularity of fantasy football possible. In the dark ages of the early '90s, before the Internet became mainstream, one poor league member had to spend ten to fifteen hours tallying everything up and distributing printouts to everyone. That's all changed with the click of a key.

Everything is now done on the computer. Thanks to the Internet managing your team, accessing statistics and checking the standings is a breeze. There are many Web sites—some, like Yahoo, that are even free—that can run your league, create a schedule, run your draft, and keep track of everything. Often these sites have chat rooms and posting forums so you can converse with other owners. They also allow you to hold live online drafts.

OVERVIEW

Fantasy football is even easier to play online because you don't have to deal with the logistics of travel. While it can be more impersonal, you also have the opportunity to compete against people from around the country. Many owners, including myself, play in both face-to-face leagues and online leagues. The technology has become so sophisticated, it has become easy to conduct live drafts online. Both beginners and experts can select their team in a short period of time. Yahoo, for instance, has free online public and private leagues. Anyone can join a public league until it fills up. Private leagues require a password.

There are advantages to participating in both online leagues and face-to-face leagues. There's nothing like renewing old ties with long-standing league members in face-to-face leagues. It's a shared interest and special kinship only those involved in fantasy football can relate to. It's hard to share that same communication online and it's exciting to be a part of a live draft where you can look at people and interact.

Drafting online has its advantages, too. You don't have to dress up or leave the house. You're in a relaxed setting and can even be doing other things, although I would not recommend that. Online drafts often go a lot faster. Many have a one-minute time limit. If you haven't made your pick by then, the interface system automatically gives you the highest-rated player left.

That's why it is always a good idea to rank players ahead of time if doing an online draft. This is a draft feature where you rank each player starting with who you believe is the number one pick all the way to the last player if you so choose. This is kind of like insurance. If something should go wrong, such as your computer crashing, you'd at least have some of the players you thought should be ranked highest. Many online draft systems offer this feature.

Another neat feature with online drafts is seeing your team's roster immediately go up on the Web site. In face-to-face leagues, it's often up to the commissioner to input everybody's team into a stat company's Web site. That can take a couple of days depending on your commissioner.

Costs of Joining

There are many types of fantasy football leagues with different formats, scoring options, and pay scales. Entry fees to join a fantasy football league range from being free, such as the Yahoo and ESPN sites, all the way up to "high-end" money leagues. The lesser-cost pay leagues can cost from $25 to $200 to enter, while the medium-cost ones might be in the $250-$600 range. One of the Internet leagues I competed in during 2004, the National Fantasy Football Championship, had a $1,250 entry fee with a $100,000 first-place payout. They held simultaneous drafts in Las Vegas, New York, and Chicago. Another league has a $1,450 entrance fee and awards $200,000 to the winner.

CBS SportsLine.com, which teamed up with NFL.com—the official fantasy football site of the NFL—had around ninety-eight thousand paid fantasy football leagues in 2004, consisting of approximately 1.3 million fantasy football teams. ESPN.com, which launched fantasy football in 1995, generated more than two million in signups for its fantasy leagues. Yahoo Sports logged some three million fantasy football users. Popular publications such as *Sports Illustrated* and *The Sporting News* also have set up fantasy leagues. These figures are all projected to go upward as more and more people get comfortable going online.

Before the Internet, traditional fantasy football leagues were composed of groups of friends, relatives, and coworkers. Everybody knew each other. Some of these leagues still remain in place. It's not uncommon for those owners who have moved away from the group to fly in from out-of-state so they can be there for their league's draft.

One Las Vegas fantasy owner, for instance, still competes in a league in Michigan and flies to Ann Arbor each season for his league's annual draft. I say airlines should begin awarding extra frequent flyer bonus points to out-of-town fantasy football owners making a pilgrimage back to their league's draft.

Getting Started

Getting into fantasy football couldn't be simpler. You can sign up with one of the many sites you could easily find on the Internet, join an existing league, or even start your own league, setting it up on the Internet or face-to-face with family and friends. If you're new to fantasy football and want to join in the fun, just go to a search engine such as google.com, and type in "fantasy football leagues," and you'll be off and running.

On the next page is a list of some of the popular fantasy football Web sites currently available on the Internet. Most are free, but some have pay areas.

This is not meant to be a comprehensive choice, but it will get you started if you're not already a member of a league. Remember new leagues start all the time. With so many choices, you shouldn't have a problem finding at least one league that fits your budget and the kind of playing style you prefer.

As fantasy football keeps growing, more and more leagues are forming each year, with fantasy participants competing in an average of 2.5 leagues each.

One Web site that could be extremely helpful, www.footballguys.com, has a ton of links and information on everything related to fantasy football.

**Popular Fantasy
Football Web sites**

1. CBSSportsline.com
2. Covers.com
3. Draftsharks.com
4. Draftzone.com
5. ESPN.com
6. Fanball.com
7. Fantasyfootballcafe.com
8. Fantasyindex.com
9. Fantasysports.yahoo.com
10. Footballguys.com
11. Footballinjuries.com
12. Insiderfootballnews.com
13. KFFL.com
14. Mr.fantasy.com
15. MSNBC.MSN.com
16. MSN.Foxsports.com
17. NFL.com
18. NFL.scout.com
19. ProFootballWeekly.com
20. Rotoworld.com
21. Sportingnews.com
22. SportsIllustrated.CNN.com
23. Thehuddle.com
24. Theredzone.org
25. USAToday.com

3. BASIC RULES

In fantasy football, you become an **owner** of a team of real NFL players that you pick before the actual season starts. You begin by obtaining a set amount of players that you feel will put up the highest number of points based on various statistical categories. Depending on the league you participate in, you acquire these players through either a draft, where owners take turns choosing players, or though an auction, where you start with a preset budget, and bid against competing owners to get the players you choose. In an auction, when you run out of money, you cannot acquire more players. And in a draft, when the drafting rounds are over, that's your team.

Once a team is assembled, you wait for the season to begin and hope that the players you chose do well. There are various scoring systems used to determine your success on the field, but we will cover them later, in the scoring section.

Your goal is to win your fantasy football league championship by accumulating points that your players earn by their performance each week. Your season follows that of the NFL, only in fantasy football, it is not how well a real team does that determines your success, but how well the individual players you chose for your team perform. It's all about the stats they post on the boards. The better they do; the better you do, again, according to the scoring system of your league.

Rosters are usually composed of a starting quarterback, two starting running backs, three starting wide receivers, one starting tight end, a starting kicker, a starting defense, and an additional starter at the flex or utility spot. Most leagues play a team defense, not individuals. That means the defense as a whole gets credit when any of its players gets points in the defensive categories. These can include interceptions, fumble recoveries, sacks and tackles.

In leagues that use individual defensive players, any defensive player can be chosen. The individual defensive positions are lineman, linebackers and defensive backs. If the league has a further breakdown, defensive ends and defensive tackles are considered linemen and safeties and cornerbacks are considered defensive backs. Linebackers are linebackers whether they play inside or outside. Most leagues limit your flex position player to being a running back, wide receiver, or tight end. In addition, depending on your league format, you have three to seven bench spots. This is where you store your backup quarterback and other reserves.

You can change your roster by a **free agent pickup**, in which you select a player who isn't on someone else's roster by **dropping** a player on your team, **making a trade** with another owner, or by picking someone on the waiver wire. The **waiver wire** is similar to the free agent pool, except it contains players who were cut during the past week by an owner in your league. If a waiver wire player isn't claimed within a week, he goes into the general free agent pool. Some leagues don't distinguish between the free agent pool and waiver wire.

Not all the players on your team "play" each week. Before whatever deadline your league has for announcing your players, you will choose a starting lineup from among your roster of players to compete. Some of the players on your teams will "sit on the bench," and their statistics will not count. Who you choose to play might be influenced by weather conditions, injuries, whether your players are affected by a bye week, team match-ups, or other factors that may influence your players' stats. You operate just like an actual NFL coach, starting players you believe will put up the best numbers.

SEVEN BASICS OF FANTASY FOOTBALL

You can summarize basic fantasy football rules in seven steps. We'll cover these steps in more detail later on.

Step #1. Assemble a league

If it's a head-to-head league, where you compete against an individual team each week, you need to have an even number of teams so that teams always have someone to compete against. Many leagues are comfortable with ten or twelve teams. That seems to be the standard number, although you can play with as few or as many teams as you like.

Step #2. Decide on the rules and size of rosters

There are many variations in how points are earned, with each league having its own preferences. For example, the number of points earned for a touchdown depends on which position scores it— for example, a receiver will get a different number of points than a quarterback for a touchdown—and that will vary from league to league. There are also variations on the number of points awarded for yardage and how defense and kickers earn points. This will all be carefully spelled out in any league you join so you know how to formulate your strategy before drafting players for your roster. And if it's a new league, you'll need to agree with the other owners on the scoring as well as each team's roster size. Roster size varies from league to league, with fifteen to seventeen players being the norm.

Step #3. Choose a commissioner

The commissioner is the person responsible for the league's constitution, enforcing the rules, and making sure the league runs smoothly.

Step #4. Set up the schedule

In head-to-head leagues, everyone should play each other at least once. If the league is large enough, you can set up divisions. On the next page is an example of how you might set up the schedule for a two-division, ten-team league.

In a Rotisserie format, statistics are compiled each week and standings are determined by adding up the number of points each team compiled in each of the categories. For example, let's say you're in a Rotisserie format twelve-team league with the categories being touchdowns, rushing yards, passing yards and receiving yards.

If you were first in touchdowns you would have twelve points, which is the maximum for that category. If you had the fewest touchdowns you would earn just one point. If you had the third highest touchdowns, you would earn ten out of twelve points.

HEAD-TO-HEAD FORMAT

Week 1: 1 vs. 10; 2 vs. 9; 3 vs. 8; 4 vs. 7; 5 vs. 6.

Week 2: 2 vs. 10; 3 vs. 1; 4 vs. 9; 5 vs. 8; 6 vs. 7.

Week 3: 3 vs. 10; 4 vs. 2; 5 vs. 1; 6 vs. 9; 7 vs. 8.

Week 4: 4 vs. 10; 5 vs. 3; 6 vs. 2; 7 vs. 1; 8 vs. 9.

Week 5: 5 vs. 10; 6 vs. 4; 7 vs. 3; 8 vs. 2; 9 vs. 1.

Week 6: 10 vs. 6; 7 vs. 5; 8 vs. 4; 9 vs. 3; 1 vs. 2.

Week 7: 10 vs. 7; 8 vs. 6; 9 vs. 5; 1 vs. 4; 2 vs. 3.

Week 8: 10 vs. 8; 9 vs. 7; 1 vs. 6; 2 vs. 5; 3 vs. 4.

Week 9: 10 vs. 9; 1 vs. 8; 2 vs. 7; 3 vs. 6; 4 vs. 5.

Week 10: 10 vs. 1; 9 vs. 2; 8 vs. 3; 7 vs. 4; 6 vs. 5.

Week 11: 10 vs. 2; 1 vs. 3; 9 vs. 4; 8 vs. 5; 7 vs. 6.

Week 12: 10 vs. 3; 2 vs. 4; 1 vs. 5; 9 vs. 6; 8 vs. 7.

Week 13: 10 vs. 4; 3 vs. 5; 2 vs. 6; 1 vs. 7; 9 vs. 8.

Week 14: 10 vs. 5; 4 vs. 6; 3 vs. 7; 2 vs. 8; 1 vs. 9.

Week 15: 6 vs. 10; 5 vs. 7; 4 vs. 8; 3 vs. 9; 2 vs. 1

Week 16: Playoffs

(No. 1 seed vs. No. 4 seed; No. 2 seed vs. No. 3 seed)

Week 17: Championship game

(between two semifinal winners)

BASIC RULES

Step #5. Hold your draft or auction

Now you choose your players either by draft or by auction, which we'll cover later, and form your fantasy football team. Prime drafting dates are the last weekend in August and the first week in September. Once you have your team, you wait for football season to begin!

Step #6. Compile your scores

When the NFL season begins, so does the fantasy football season. You hope to earn as many points as you can. The better your players do statistically, the more points you earn. Week by week, you watch your team—and your opponent's teams—to see how they perform on the field. Points can be charted by the league commissioner or secretary. There are also commissioner services available on the Internet that handle this for free or at an affordable price.

There are Yahoo and ESPN leagues will compile your scores for free and about 100 pay sites that can compile stats for you, including: tqstats.com, cbs.sportsline.com, cdmsports.com, antsports.com, fantasyfootballcommissio ner.com, statsworld.com, and commissioneronline.com.

Step #7. Transactions

Some of your players may get injured and others may underperform. Your goal is to win, so during the season you make moves, including picking up free agents, cutting players, and making deals with fellow owners.

Step #8. The Playoffs

If you've compiled a good enough won-lost record,

or accumulated enough total points on the season, to be one of the top teams in your league, you get to enter the playoffs. In head-to-head leagues, which are the most popular format, the top two or four teams compete in the playoffs, which consist of anywhere from one to three weeks in length.

Step #9. The Championship

The winner of the playoffs—just as in the NFL—is crowned the champion.

Step #10. Celebrate

If you're the champion, celebrate your hard-earned victory with a great night out!

There are various ways to accumulate points and different systems on how to win your league. Let's look at these now.

SCORING SYSTEMS

While there is no standard scoring system used in all leagues for how players score points—each league uses its own point system—there is one thing common to all fantasy football leagues: points are accumulated each week during the season based on how your players perform. In other words, a player's individual performance—the statistics he puts on the board—is what matters.

For offensive players, the most popular statistical categories for earning points are touchdowns, passing yards, rushing yards, receiving yards, and kicking points. For defensive players, they are sacks, interceptions, and scoring. Some leagues even draft head coaches where you receive one point for every win your coach produces.

In head-to-head formats, where your team is matched against an opponent's team each week, the winner is determined by the team that has the highest score. Remember, your team score is an accumulation of all the points earned that week by the players on your handpicked fantasy football team. Your final tally is compared to your opponent's score. The highest total wins.

In formats where you don't go head to head against an individual team, your points accumulate from week to week, with the best totals at the end of the year determining who wins the championship.

Basic Method Leagues

The most basic type of league uses just a couple of categories, and is thus the most simple to play. An example of a basic league, which is a good format for beginners, is where anyone who scores a touchdown on your roster earns six points for your team. There are variations where running backs and receivers earn six points for a touchdown, while quarterbacks earn three or four points for a touchdown pass. Field goals are worth three points and extra points are worth one point. Defenses also can earn six points by returning an interception or fumble for a touchdown and by scoring a special teams touchdown.

Touchdowns are weighed heavily in basic leagues. The universal thing about basic leagues, and what makes them so simple, is that you mainly just need to pull for touchdowns and not be concerned with yardage figures.

Touchdowns get the most attention and are easy to follow. Touchdown specialists like power backs Jerome Bettis and T.J. Duckett are of more value in this type of league. Duckett, for instance, has averaged just 644 yards rushing during 2003 and 2004, but has scored nineteen touchdowns in this two-year span. Bettis enters the 2005 season having not rushed for 1,000 yards the past three years. However, he's scored a combined twenty-nine touchdowns during 2002-2004.

Performance Method Leagues

Unlike the basic league premise, which mainly rewards touchdowns, performance leagues also count various yardage figures such as passing yards, rushing yards, and receiving yards, along with different defensive statistics. All of these statistics count for each of your starters, and decide the total points you accumulate for the week and season.

Performance method leagues are the most widely played leagues, and for my money, the most fun. There is a lot more skill in choosing your players and following the games, and there are so many variances and nuances in the scoring system each league sets up, that you would be hard-pressed to find two leagues with the exact same set of scoring rules.

Performance League Scoring

Many performance leagues count one point for every 10 yards rushing and receiving a player in your starting lineup gets, and one point for every 25 yards passing. This is done to try to balance out the positions and categories, trying to make each skill position of equal importance. Running backs have always been the dominant position, so some leagues award one point for every reception made by a wide receiver or tight end, while giving just a half point to a running back for every catch he makes.

There are leagues that break down statistics even further, awarding 1.5 points for 15 yards rushing, or 1.9 points if a player ends up with 19 yards rushing. It's similar with kickers. Instead of earning three points for any field goal, some leagues break it down to where a kicker would score 4.7 points for you instead of 3 if he were to make a 47-yard field goal. If he made a 27-yard field, you would get 2.7 points instead of 3 points in this type of scoring system.

Bonus points are given out in some leagues. These can be earned by 300-yard passing figures, 100-yard rushing games, and 100-yard receiving games.

Below are some examples of how each position can score in standard performance leagues. Remember that the basic method leagues use a more simplified method of scoring, mostly based on actual points scored, with touchdowns being the main statistical category and yardage gained being unimportant.

Quarterbacks	Points
Touchdown pass or run	4
25 yards passing	1
10 yards rushing	1
Passing or rushing two-point touchdown conversion	1

Let's say your quarterback threw for 250 yards and two touchdowns while rushing for 20 yards. That would be worth 18 points. The two TD passes add up to eight points. The 250 yards figure out to eight points, and the 20 rushing yards add up to two points, giving you a total of 18.

Running Backs	Points
Touchdown*	6
10 yards rushing	1
10 yards receiving	1
Catching a pass	1/2
Scoring on a two-point conversion	2
* either by rushing, receiving or passing	

If your running back rushed for 83 yards, scored one TD, and caught two passes for 23 yards, your total would be 17 points. The TD would be worth six, the 83 yards on the ground would count for eight points, the two receptions would be worth one point, since each catch counts half a point, and the 23 receiving yards would be worth two points, adding up to 17.

Receivers: Wide Receivers and Tight Ends	Points
Touchdown*	6
10 yards receiving	1
10 yards rushing	1
Catching a pass	1
Scoring on a two-point conversion	2

*either receiving or rushing

So if your receiver happened to catch a TD pass, haul in seven passes for 77 yards, and also score on a two-point conversion, you would earn 22 points. The breakdown would be six points for the TD, seven points for the seven receptions, seven points for the 77 yards, and two for catching a two-point conversion following a touchdown.

The Titans' Drew Bennett nearly single-handedly won some fantasy owners their Week 14 match of the 2004 season when he hauled in twelve passes against the Chiefs for 233 yards and three touchdowns. That was worth 53 points, not including any bonus points Bennett would have earned for his owner in leagues awarding bonus figures. The three scores were worth 18 points. The twelve receptions counted for 12 points and the 233 yards factored in an additional 23 points for a total of 53.

Billy Volek, Bennett's quarterback for that game, also had a monster outing, throwing for 426 yards and four touchdowns.

That was worth 35 points, with the four touchdowns counting for 16 points (four points for each TD) and the 426 yards counting for 17 points (one point for every 25 yards). In addition, Volek rushed for 24 yards, which was worth two points (one point for every 10 yards rushing). Volek's fantasy points for the week would be even higher in leagues awarding bonus points for multiple touchdowns and passing yards.

Kickers	Points
Field goal	3
Extra point	1

If a kicker makes three field goals and three extra points, he scores 12 points for you. The frustration comes in if your kicker's team puts up 42 points on six touchdowns with no field goals. If your kicker makes all six extra points, he finishes with only six points. This is easily matched by an opposing team's kicker making two field goals. You can have all kinds of variations with kickers such as subtracting points for every missed kick, and giving added points for longer field goals.

Using this criteria, if your defense held an opponent to nine points (worth seven fantasy points), while getting three interceptions (worth six fantasy points with each

BASIC RULES

interception counting two), two fumble recoveries (worth four fantasy points), and five sacks (one fantasy point for each sack), you would earn 22 points.

Defense	Points
Touchdown*	6
Holding a team scoreless	10
Holding a team under 10 points	7
Getting a safety	5
Getting an interception	2
Recovering a fumble	2
Getting a sack	1

*any type of touchdown scored by the defense or special teams

There are many other categories you can use to score points, although these can get quite technical. For a quarterback they can be completions, yards per completion, or completion percentage. For a running back they can be average yards per rush and number of carries. For receivers it can be yards per reception. You can add multiple categories on defense such as yards allowed, sack yards, number of points allowed, and yards per play.

Some leagues penalize for negative plays such as an interception, fumble, or missed field goal. Usually the penalty is minus one point for each interception and fumble. On missed field goals, it is minus one for a missed field goal of 40 or more yards, minus two for a missed field goal of 30 or more yards, and minus three for a missed extra point or field goal of less than 30 yards. There have been cases of an owner losing his head-to-head match by one point because his kicker finished with negative points. Ouch.

Here is my team's scoring breakdown from Week 5 of the 2004 season, when I won a narrow victory. The league format for a starting lineup was one quarterback, two running backs, three wide receivers, one tight end, one team defense, one kicker, and one player (either a running back, wide receiver, or tight end) at flex.

WEEK 5, 2004 SEASON CHART

Quarterback: Brett Favre - 2 TD passes, 338 passing yards. **Total:** 26 points (six points for each TD pass, one point for every 25 passing yards).

Running Back: Travis Henry – 33 yards rushing. **Total:** Three points (one point for every 10 yards rushing).

Running Back: Lee Suggs – 30 yards rushing, 20 yards receiving on two receptions. **Total:** Six points (three points for the 30 rushing, two points for the 20 receiving yards, and one point for the two receptions with a running back receiving half a point per reception).

Wide Receiver: Randy Moss – Two touchdowns, five passes caught for 90 yards. **Total:** 26 points (12 for the two TDs, nine for the 90 receiving yards and five for the five receptions with the league format being one point for each pass caught by a wide receiver and tight end).

Wide Receiver: Keyshawn Johnson – One touchdown, four passes caught for 43 yards. **Total:** 14 points (six points for the TD, four points for the 43 receiving yards, and four points for the four receptions).

Wide Receiver: Eric Moulds – Six passes caught for 54 yards. **Total:** 11 points (six points for the six receptions and five points for the 54 yards).

Tight End: Boo Williams – One touchdown, two passes caught for 24 yards. **Total:** 10 points (six for the TD, two for the two passes caught, and two for the 24 receiving yards).

Kicker: Josh Brown – Two field goals and three extra points. **Total:** 10 points (four points for one field goal of 40 or more yards, three points for one field goal of 30 or more yards, and three points for three extra point kicks).

Defense: Patriots – Three sacks, one interception, one fumble recovery. **Total:** Five points (one point for every sack, interception, and fumble recovery).

Flex: Antonio Bryant (wide receiver) – One pass caught for 15 yards. **Total:** Two points (one point for the reception and one point for the 15 yards).

The key for me in this matchup was getting a huge game from my number one pick, Randy Moss, along with a big performance from my quarterback, Brett Favre. My running backs had terrible performances, but my receivers made up for it scoring 63 of my 112 points. I was fortunate that in this league, receptions by wide receivers and tight ends counted for one point. This allowed me to pick up 18 points as Moss, Johnson, Moulds, Williams, and Bryant combined for 18 receptions.

4. STARTING A LEAGUE

To start a league, all you need to do is assemble a group of owners, usually anywhere from eight to sixteen, choose a commissioner, and decide on a set of rules. Probably the most popular leagues contain ten to twelve owners. It gets tough drafting, especially for those with the last pick in the first round, if you have more owners in a league, because not every owner is assured of getting a superstar in the first round like they would in leagues of eight to ten.

PLAYING FOR CASH PRIZES

In a league where each player pays to enter, each owner pays a set fee at the beginning. There is also a fee for each transaction made, such as a trade or free agent pickup. This keeps the pot growing. When the season ends, the total pot is distributed to those who finished in the money. Usually the top three or four places collect, with the winner taking home 50 percent of the pot, second place collecting 25 percent, third place getting 15 percent, and fourth place earning 10 percent.

Some leagues are just for fun, and will give the winner a trophy. Many leagues involve money, although most are low-dollar leagues. The main purpose of participating in fantasy football is for enjoyment and to have fun, not to get rich. It's sort of like a neighborhood poker game in that it is fun to play and compete, but you need the lure of a financial payoff as an additional reward.

DIFFERENT TYPES OF LEAGUES
There are various types of leagues available—head-to-head, Rotisserie, salary cap, and keeper leagues—and we'll go over them in this section.

Head-to-Head League
In a **head-to-head** league, which is the most popular style played, you compete directly against one opposing owner's team, much as two football teams compete directly against one another in the NFL. The team scoring the most points wins that week's "game." Also like the NFL, you play a different team each week. When all the games for that week are finished, you add up the points and the team with the highest total wins.

The regular season in head-to-head fantasy leagues usually lasts twelve to fourteen weeks. You then have your fantasy playoffs during the final two or three weeks of the real NFL season. This consists of the top two or four teams competing. Many leagues schedule their championship game on the second-to-last week of the NFL season. Teams that have clinched a division title or playoff spot often hold out their star players so that they can avoid injuries or rest up for the playoffs.

One week you could win scoring 40 points, while in another week you could lose scoring 135 points. All you can do is try to field the best possible team. You have no control over your opponent. You can put up the second-most points in your league that week and still lose.

Here's an example of what a head-to-head scoring format might look like. This was taken from my 2004 Week 1 match when my team, the Sleeping Koalas, played a team called Nip Tuck in the head-to-head National Fantasy Football Championship League:

-SLEEPING KOALAS-

QB—Brett Favre 13.05 points

RB—William Green 11. 2 points

RB—Travis Henry 9.9 points

WR—Randy Moss 20.55 points

WR—Eric Moulds 20.5 points

WR—Keyshawn Johnson 20.1 points

TE—Boo Williams 3.3 points

Def—New England 7 points

K—Josh Brown 3 points

Flex—Richie Anderson 5.1 points

Total points: 113.7

-NIP TUCK-
QB—Matt Hasselbeck 17.2 points
RB—Clinton Portis 24.3 points
RB—Kevin Jones 7.5 points
WR—Torry Holt 16.6 points
WR—Corey Bradford 5.4 points
WR—Plaxico Burress 2.3 points
TE—Itula Mili 2.5 points
Def—Indianapolis 6 points
K—Ryan Longwell 7.1 points
Flex—Ashley Lelie 12.8 points
Total points 101.7

This particular matchup was won at the wide receiver position. Even though my opponent outscored me at quarterback, running back, kicker, and flex, my three wide receivers and tight end outscored his by a margin of 64.9 points to 26.5 points.

Head-to-head competition can get nerve-racking. Sometimes the matches are extremely close and are not decided until the end of the Monday night game. I still vividly recall dining and drinking Hefeweizen at an upscale brewery with my boss and four professional football bettors in Las Vegas during a Monday night in mid-October while the Buccaneers-Rams game was on.

Now some of these guys had big money riding on this game. I had more at stake—my fantasy opponent had Bucs' wide receiver Michael Clayton and I only had a medium-sized lead and no players involved. The rest of the table didn't seem to care too much about the game, although they certainly had one eye on the set while they talked.

Clayton, who was on my opponent's team, was making catches and catches and catches. It was agony. Finally I had to excuse myself and walk away, but not before letting out an embarrassing shriek after Clayton hauled in his eighth reception, pushing him above 140 yards and giving my opponent enough points to overtake me.

In a room full of professionals, I had been exposed as an amateur, unable to keep my emotions in check and accept defeat. I don't blame Clayton for my outburst. It's this damn head-to-head format. People like it, though, because it's easy. That particular week I put up the fourth-most points of the fourteen owners and lost.

Each loss can be painful if you dwell on plays that cost you a victory. The week I lost to the Clayton owner, I had Randy Moss sit out the second half with a hamstring injury, his first injury ever in the NFL. In another loss, the officials didn't give Travis Henry a touchdown against the Raiders when he clearly was in the end zone. When my quarterback, Brett Favre, missed the fourth quarter I dropped another head-to-head matchup by one point.

Every owner who narrowly loses can recite these types of bad beats. It's almost like a badge of honor to top your fellow owner on your bad beat stories. Sometimes it works the other way and you win when your players don't perform well and your opponent's team has an off day.

But try finding an owner who says he has had more good luck than bad. He doesn't exist.

Invariably you're going to lose when your team plays well and that's what you remember most. It's also a given that there will be some lucky owner who doesn't have nearly the points you do, but is much higher up in the standings. It's always irritating, too, to lose because some owner uses a player that has no business being a starter. Naturally that's the one week where that player proceeds to have a big game.

I remember smiling upon seeing my opponent in Week 3 of the 2001 season use up one of his wide receiver spots on Terance Mathis of the Falcons. Mathis was nearing the end of his career. He managed to play every game that season, but never had more than 70 receiving yards and only scored two touchdowns. However, both those touchdowns came in Week 3.

That's part of the charm of the head-to-head format. It can be agonizing, but it can feel so good when you win. Unlike daily sports such as baseball and basketball, you don't have to spend time each day pouring over your roster. You can spend as little as five minutes a week setting or tweaking the lineup you feel will give you the most points for that week. There are weeks, especially when none of your players are affected by having a bye, where you can just stick with your typical lineup.

Other times, though, you need to make one or two slight changes such as switching your number three wide receiver or putting in a new player at your utility spot in order to take advantage of those players going against weaker defenses that week.

STARTING A LEAGUE

Rotisserie League

In a **Rotisserie** format, which is used in some leagues, you keep a running total on every category each week. For instance, in a twelve-team setup you would get 12 points in rushing if you had the most rushing yards all the way to the lowest team getting one point. There are no head-to-head matches. At the end of the season the team with the highest overall total wins.

This is my preferred format, although this type of league can be harder to find. Both of my face-to-face, twelve-owner Las Vegas leagues use this style. We use the standard categories (touchdowns, passing yards, receiving yards, rushing yards, and kicking), but we also added tackles and sacks to stay up on individual defensive players, too.

If you accumulate the most passing yards, for instance, you get 12 points. It goes all the way down to the last place person in the category getting one point. Each category is scored the same. So in a twelve-team league with seven categories, a perfect score would be 84 points. If you finished last in all seven categories, you would end up with seven points.

Here is how the final 2004 standings looked in my twelve-team Rotisserie league, which we named the "Low Rollers League."

2004 LOW ROLLERS LEAGUE STANDINGS

Name	Points
1. Rick	66
2. Stephen	62
3. Scott	57
4. Rex	52
5. Fred	49
6. Frank	48.5
7. Smitty	48
8. Tim	42
9. Al	34
10. Dave	30
11. Barry	29.5
12. Buzz	28

-TOUCHDOWNS-

1. Rick	229
2. Rex	216
3. Smitty	185
4. Stephen	184
5. Scott	183
6. Fred	165
7. Frank	164
8. Barry	158
9. Tim	154
10. Al	147
11. Dave	130
12. Buzz	127

-PASSING YARDS-

1. Rick 10,117
2. Dave 10,110
3. Smitty 9,471
4. Stephen 9,150
5. Tim 8,784
6. Rex 8,657
7. Barry 8,222
8. Fred 7,934
9. Scott 7,313
10. Al 7,201
11. Frank 6,636
12. Buzz 6,427

-RUSHING YARDS-

1. Rick 5,048
2. Scott 4,906
3. Stephen 4,519
4. Frank 4,225
5. Fred 4,190
6. Tim 4,077
7. Smitty 3,972
8. Rex 3,686
9. Al 3,333
10. Dave 3,041
11. Buzz 2,885
12. Barry 2,678

-RECEIVING YARDS-

1. Scott   5,997
2. Fred   5,370
3. Stephen   5,356
4. Frank   5,313
5. Rick   5,263
6. Smitty   5,199
7. Tim   5,026
8. Barry   4,862
9. Rex   4,766
10. Al   4,337
11. Buzz   4,261
12. Dave   4,070

-KICKING POINTS-

1. Rex   293
2. Frank   270
3. Stephen   267
4. Rick   260
5. Scott   256
6. Smitty   248
7. Buzz   231
8. Al   230
9. Dave   219
10. Fred (tie) 215
11. Barry (tie) 215
12. Tim   191

STARTING A LEAGUE

-TACKLES-

1. Rex   515
2. Stephen   504
3. Buzz   501
4. Rick   479
5. Barry   472
6. Scott   470
7. Fred   469
8. Tim   459
9. Al   445
10. Smitty   426
11. Frank   389
12. Dave   264

-SACKS-

1. Al   55
2. Tim   37
3. Frank   35.5
4. Fred (tie) 35.5
5. Dave   34
6. Scott   33.5
7. Buzz   30
8. Smitty   28.5
9. Rick   26
10. Stephen   21
11. Barry   19.5
12. Rex   14

STARTING A LEAGUE

-TACKLES-

1. Rex   515
2. Stephen   504
3. Buzz   501
4. Rick   479
5. Barry   472
6. Scott   470
7. Fred   469
8. Tim   459
9. Al   445
10. Smitty   426
11. Frank   389
12. Dave   264

-SACKS-

1. Al   55
2. Tim   37
3. Frank   35.5
4. Fred (tie) 35.5
5. Dave   34
6. Scott   33.5
7. Buzz   30
8. Smitty   28.5
9. Rick   26
10. Stephen   21
11. Barry   19.5
12. Rex   14

Rick won the league, edging me out in the final week, by finishing first in passing yards, rushing yards, and touchdowns. He received 12 out of 12 points in each of those categories. He also scored nine points in the kicking and tackles categories by placing fourth in each one and added eight points in receiving yards, placing fifth, and rounded out his total by scoring four points in the sacks category. This gave him a combined total of 66 points.

In the long run, the best team usually wins because you're taking the entire season into account. The top four teams cash. There are no playoffs with this format. It is straight seventeen weeks—just the way I like it. There is no championship matchup being decided in Week 16 or Week 17 when players largely responsible for your record could be resting because their team already had clinched a division title.

Those who rode Terrell Davis to their league championship game in 1997 remain the poster owners for this bad beat. Davis rushed for 1,757 yards and scored fifteen touchdowns that season. However, he carried just ten times for 28 yards in Week 16, and then Mike Shanahan held him out entirely the final week of the regular season. Davis proceeded to rush for 184, 101, 139, and 157 yards in the post-season, scoring eight touchdowns in the process and leading the Broncos to a Super Bowl title. That was no consolation for the Davis owners whose playoff format came on Weeks 16 and 17.

You have some flexibility with the Rotisserie scoring system and can try different strategies. One of our owners, for instance, keeps ignoring the passing category, choosing not to draft any starting quarterback. Instead he loads up on running backs and is the first to grab kickers. This strategy is too risky for my taste, because if you give up on one category, you're forced to finish high in all the others. Unfortunately for this owner, touchdowns are a category and kickers can't be counted on. It's no coincidence that he's yet to finish in the money.

Balance is Essential

The key to winning in this format is balance. You don't need to win a category by an overwhelming margin. My goal is to finish second in every category, or if I have to finish first, to just barely be above the second place team. I want to be balanced, to place well in all categories. Usually anywhere from 58-66 points is good enough to win the league. I won the league in '97 and '99 accumulating 68 points each year. That's been the highest total. The lowest winning total was 56 points. The median winning total the past seven years is 64.

Let me illustrate what I mean. One of our owners loves wide receivers. A couple of years ago he made Randy Moss and Marvin Harrison his first two picks. He easily captured the receiving yards category, but failed to finish in the money. He couldn't produce enough passing and rushing yards.

Another owner once won rushing by more than 900 yards. He didn't place in the top four in the final standings either. He holds our league's all-time record for most rushing yards. However, you can't win a fantasy football title unless you finish well in the other categories, too.

You need enough strong players at each position to score well in every category.

SALARY CAP LEAGUE

The **salary cap** league is sometimes used by companies, products, or Web sites that offer a fantasy football contest. You pick your players from a preexisting salary range. You fill your team any way you want, but can't go above a set salary cap limit. So if you choose Daunte Culpepper, Randy Moss, and LaDainian Tomlinson—who all cost a lot of money—you won't have much money left to buy other superstars.

An example of this format is *The Sporting News* Basic Salary Cap Football, where you're given a $35,000 budget in which to choose seven players—two quarterbacks, two running backs, two wide receivers, and a defense. The highest score for that week wins. The following week you start again with $35,000. You're not allowed to carry over any unused salary, so if you only spent $30,000 the week before, that unused $5,000 goes to waste. You can keep some of your players or buy an all-new lineup. Sometimes the league increases or decreases salaries on players depending on the kind of season they are having.

I competed in this type of league once, winning a SportsLine Experts league back in 1997. My partner was oddsmaker Russ Culver of the syndicated Glantz/Culver betting line. Since both of us were in Vegas at the time, we called our team "Siegfried and Roy." Luckily, we didn't run into any team named the "White Tigers."

Handicapping matchups is instrumental in doing well with this type of league structure, since you're often allowed to pick a new team each week as long as you don't exceed the salary cap. We just made sure the superstars we selected were in good situations against weak defenses, while filling the rest of our roster with solid players who also were in favorable matchups that week.

I never cared much for this type of league, though. There's something about seeing my opponent have the same players as I have in his lineup that takes the fun out of it. Budgeting becomes huge. There's rarely any reason to dig deep in the talent pool or gamble when you can set up a safe, solid lineup by not going overboard with salary on a superstar. It doesn't take a whole lot of brainpower.

Some contests have you pick from prearranged talent pools. Beginners may enjoy this style because it's a simple way of being introduced to fantasy football.

KEEPER LEAGUE

This kind of league is just as the name implies. In a **keeper** league you can carry over a certain number of players each year. These are your **keepers**. Non-keeper leagues don't retain any players from the previous year. Everybody starts new each season in non-keeper leagues.

The format in keeper leagues can be head-to-head or Rotisserie style. Players are obtained through a draft or auction. Being in a keeper league makes you feel like a real owner. That's one of the pluses. You get a sense of continuity in a league where you can retain some of your players, and do it without any labor woes. In typical keeper leagues, you can protect from three to seven players for up to three years. Drafts and auction take less time because teams are already stocked with players.

Another nice thing about keeper leagues is that owners stay motivated all season. Some owners in non-keeper leagues will lose interest and not stay competitive if their team isn't doing well. There's nothing for them to play for, so they essentially all but drop out. That doesn't happen nearly as often in keeper leagues, because an owner can play for the following year. So he remains active, looking to trade and pick up players in free agency with an eye toward the following season. He always has incentive.

There's a strong commitment from owners in keeper leagues. It's almost a privilege to be in one. Owners are in it for the long haul. When you have players you're carrying over, you think more about football year round. You're interested in any off-season news, minicamps, and of course, training camp, paying particularly close attention to your roster as you prepare to decide which players to keep or throw back.

Having a balanced team is just as important in winning a keeper league as in non-keeper leagues. In our first auction league in 2003, I sunk most of my allotted dollars into running backs, buying Ricky Williams, Stephen Davis, Tiki Barber, and Fred Taylor. Near the three-quarter mark of the season I had the rushing yards category already wrapped up.

STARTING A LEAGUE

So, desperate to unload my runners, I just about gave away Williams and Davis in trades, but I did get two undervalued keepers for the following year, plus a top sack guy, and still easily won rushing. Unfortunately, one of those so-called keepers was a three dollar Michael Bennett, who got hurt right before the 2004 season and ended up playing very little.

Like most things, there are good and bad points about keeper leagues. One obvious detriment is there are fewer stars to draft. If you're in a ten-team league where everybody can protect up to four players, you could be missing out on forty good players, many of whom are probably running backs. That really thins out the running back crop. It might be years before certain players become available again to the rest of the league. That's a good argument for not being able to retain a player more than two or three years in a keeper league.

Another minus is lopsided trades. It's rare to find one owner totally ripping off another in non-keeper leagues. Each wants to win *that* season. Goals can be different in keeper leagues. One owner might be trying to win this season, while another owner has given up and is targeting the following year. The owner who has given up may, for example, have a superstar running back. However, that running back is hurt, or in the final year of his keeper status contract, meaning he can't be protected next season. So that star running back isn't much good to the owner. So he trades him to another owner, who is trying to win the current season. In return he receives a couple of draft choices, or a promising player. The trade is definitely slanted and one-sided toward the owner in contention getting the superstar runner. But the other owner—who hopefully shopped the running back to all league members trying to get the best deal—at least gets something for a player he no longer can hold on to.

These types of deals, while understandable, can cause hard feelings among league members. Being in both keeper and non-keeper leagues, I notice a lot more trading and free agent moves in keeper leagues. That means an increased pot and plenty of activity.

5. PREPARING FOR YOUR SEASON

There really is no complete off-season when it comes to fantasy football. February and March are the quiet months, but you should never stop paying attention. You need to stay on top of where prominent free agents go once the season ends, and how this might increase or decrease their fantasy statistics. Minicamps in May and June are a good time, too, to get an early indication of who is in shape, which players are still rehabbing an injury, who is holding out and potential sleepers.

DRAFT RESEARCH

Information is the ammunition you need for your draft. Lack of information isn't the problem. Too much information is. You need to find enough time to do the necessary homework. Actually, don't call it homework—that word has a negative connotation. Researching your fantasy football draft should be fun. If it isn't, maybe you need to examine your motives for being in fantasy football.

In late April, right around the time of the NFL draft, I start reenergizing the fantasy football battery for the upcoming season. Ease back into your research. Many fans get their news from mainstream sources. They watch ESPN and read their local paper or *USA Today*. Some also subscribe to *Sports Illustrated* or *The Sporting News*. Then they buy several fantasy football magazines close to draft time. This amount of research is fine for the average fantasy participant. He's putting time in and gathering enough information to compete. He certainly knows more than the average person. It's from these outlets that perceptions on players and teams are developed. You certainly need to be aware of what's being said, read, and heard in these general media outlets.

But if you're serious about winning, you need to have additional information sources. Information is the main weapon in fantasy football. Those with the best weapons have an edge.

Let's look at the various places where you can learn more about fantasy football.

TV and Radio

You can now watch football twenty-four hours a day with the launching of the NFL network. Their roundtable discussion shows can be informative and offer a wide range of opinions. HBO's "Inside the NFL" is a good show. I especially enjoy listening to Bob Costas and Cris Collinsworth.

You can catch football guests on the radio from time to time. Rarely do coaches and players say anything of significance during interviews, but sometimes you can read between the lines. The guests I most enjoying listening to are information people like Chris Mortensen, Peter King, John Clayton, and Mel Kiper. It's their job to be up on the latest information and to impart that knowledge without bias. One of the better radio shows is hosted by Clayton and Sean Salisbury. They talk football for three hours. If you can get past their annoying and forced style of ripping each other, their information is often quite good.

Magazines

Even during the off-season there are fantasy football magazines to be found. Looking at one gets the competitive juices flowing again, while also providing a handy reference for last year's statistics. You can find more than a dozen magazines devoted to fantasy football on sale as the season draws closer. Many of these magazines have similar formats, rating the players at each position using their statistics from the past three years.

I like to see a player's full career statistics. For instance Muhsin Muhammad was ranked around fiftieth among wide receivers going into 2004 by many publications. That rating would be about right based on his three previous years. Muhammad had 837 receiving yards and three touchdowns in 2003. He had 823 receiving yards and three touchdowns in 2002 and 585 receiving yards and one touchdown in 2001. But if you had more than the last three years of research on Muhammad, you would have seen he had a history of producing "B" level numbers. In 1999 he had eight touchdowns and 1,253 receiving. He followed that up with 1,183 receiving yards and six scores in 2000. Going by those numbers, it shouldn't have been a total shock to see Muhammad lead the NFL with 1,405 receiving yards in 2004.

I wouldn't buy any magazine just for its player rankings. It's the analysis I'm interested in. However, magazine writers are hindered by early deadlines. So what I'm looking for is good analysis and handy reference material. I want to see each team's strength of schedule, statistics, bye week, player projections, and well-written theories that aren't too esoteric, such as if wide receivers really do experience a breakout season in their third year.

One of the strengths of a magazine is the ability and space to go in-depth on a topic. Now, with so many specialized fantasy football magazines available, it's really a buyer's market. You can see exactly what interests you. There also are the mainstream football preview magazines.

I enjoy reading *The Sporting News's* annual football preview magazine because of the analysis of offensive linemen and coaches. I also pick up *Pro Football Weekly's* annual preview to get another viewpoint and to get box scores from each game in the previous year, something most magazines don't provide.

Sports Illustrated often provides provocative opinions. I especially enjoy their preview section when they quote a scout holding nothing back in his opinions. The problem, though, with *Sports Illustrated's* preview is that it comes out so late that many fantasy drafts have already taken place.

PREPARING FOR YOUR SEASON

Using the Internet to Get an Edge

Stories on the Internet are far more up to date than magazines. Having followed sports since the early 1960s, I'm still amazed how much free information is available on the Internet. It's made researching so easy. Preparing for my fantasy drafts before the late '90s was much tougher. I remember going to the library nearly every day to check out available out-of-town newspapers. It was so tough back then to get news outside your local area. I knew of one old-time Las Vegas gambler, back in pre-Internet and ESPN days, who used to pay an airline employee to collect sports sections for him that were left on planes from passengers traveling from different parts of the country.

It's much easier nowadays. The key is having the time. Even for those like me who practically live on the Internet, you still have to pick and choose the Web sites you visit. Reading ESPN, *Sports Illustrated,* and other big sports outlets is a no-brainer. I'll also read online newspapers from all the cities where NFL teams are located. Some have multiple newspapers, so I'll scan around forty-five newspapers a day, though I don't read every article. I'll seek out certain writers, avoid others, and won't spend the time to read long feature articles, no matter how well written they might be. I don't care what kind of upbringing Corey Dillon had. I just want to know if he has enough left to produce another 1,400-yard rushing season.

If it were up to me, I'd rather read a fifteen-inch notes column full of insights than a ninety-inch award-winning feature piece. It's the same with columnists. Some are good. Some aren't worth reading. The best have the knack of entertaining while providing information. It's the same with fantasy football Web sites that have sprung up all over the place. They're fun, but they can go overboard, such as posting a twenty-inch article on why Mike Alstott makes a good sleeper fantasy pick. He doesn't. But that's another chapter.

My favorite type of fantasy article is a pro-and-con take on players, where two informed people who know how to write discuss how high the player should be drafted. Even if you strongly disagree with a viewpoint, it's good to keep an open mind. Curtis Martin is proof of that. I was sure he was on the downside of his career going into 2004. I had no interest in taking him before the fifth round no matter what anyone wrote or said. All Martin did was lead the NFL in rushing, and score double-digit touchdowns in 2004.

Each team has a Web site, too. Rarely do I check these out. It may be up-to-date, but I want my news objective without bias. Team and fan sites have too much propaganda. I don't want spin. I want truth. Is Drew Henson capable of big things in the NFL? Can Deuce McAllister be a top-five running back if he doesn't have a good fullback leading the way? Does Chad Pennington have enough arm strength to become an elite quarterback? Can the Texans defense ever be worth starting on the fantasy level? I'm not going to get these answers reading press releases or from quotes spewing the company line.

PREPARING FOR YOUR SEASON

It comes down to time, enjoyment, and bucks. Some newspapers, like the *Dallas Morning News, Atlanta Constitution, and Milwaukee Journal,* have pay areas for added NFL coverage. Being a Green Bay Packers fan, it's worth the extra dollars to pay for premium Packer content. There's so much content that is free, though, that you really don't need to shell out additional bucks.

Posting Forums

These often are found on various specialized Web sites. For instance, the Internet site I write for, Covers.com, has a posting forum with threads on fourteen different sports subjects such as football, college football, and basketball.

Posting forums can be worth reading. It comes down to the intelligence level of the posters. It's a matter of picking and choosing worthwhile threads. I enjoyed lurking through some of the topics at the National Fantasy Football Championship posting forum.

This was the posting forum for the NFFC league that had a $1,500 entry fee and awarded $100,000 to the champion. You knew these were serious participants. There were several sharp posters. Topics included various strategies and ideas, along with thoughts on different players. These posting forums also are a good way to solicit instant feedback on such matters as who makes the better keeper, which defense should be your top choice and what players are best suited to have breakout seasons.

If finding enough time is a problem, which it usually is for most people, do a condensed version of research. Try the cliff note approach of just skimming through the papers and checking out a fantasy Web site like FanBall or RotoWorld that summarizes the latest player developments and injuries with capsule summaries on the side of the page.

Personal Contact

Don't be shy about picking the brain of someone whose opinion you respect. Most successful fantasy football owners are flattered to be asked for their opinions. Many professional NFL beat writers and those specializing in fantasy football enjoy feedback. They appreciate you taking the time to e-mail. If you're ever in a position to offer them some information or story tip, it could pay dividends because, in return, they might provide some fantasy football insight down the road.

Don't become a pest, though. I had a friend of a friend who called me before the start of football asking for draft help. I spent nearly an hour on the phone preparing him. I was surprised to receive a call from him after the first week, asking what lineup he should use. Okay, not a problem. But then each week, I either received a call or e-mail from him with the same request. I finally put a halt to it the following year. When I e-mail an NFL beat writer or columnist, I try to give him or her something they might be able to use. In my job, for instance, I write about betting, point spreads, and gaming. This kind of information can make a good note or sidebar for a daily newspaper writer.

Saints fans might find it interesting, and frustrating, to know their team has failed to cover the spread hosting the Falcons nineteen of the past twenty-one years. If I pass this item to a Saints writer, then I don't feel guilty asking how Deuce McAllister's ankle is feeling this week. Writers are trying to develop their sources, too. If a person is knowledgeable and has a good opinion, I'll listen no matter what his job or title is. I actually picked up a pretty good source taking the high road with a disgruntled reader. I wrote a series of team previews for Covers.com that was picked up by MSNBC. In writing about the San Diego Chargers before the start of the 2004 season, I said they were the worst team I've ever seen on paper in the free agency era. Not one of my finer predictions as it turned out.

When the Chargers opened 7-3 I was flooded with e-mails from angry Chargers fans ripping me. It seems one Chargers fan found the article and reprinted it on a posting forum frequented by rabid Chargers backers. Years of frustration poured out, and I felt the brunt of it. I skipped the more venomous and moronic e-mails, but answered the rest, saying I certainly was wrong, but asking if anyone could honestly and realistically expect the Chargers to have done that well. They finished 12-4. Their over/under win total at sports books going into that season was 4 1/2.

One fan actually listed several reasons why he knew from the beginning the Chargers would be much improved. His reasons made sense. He follows the Chargers very closely and knows football. I'm not too proud to pick his brain regarding this team. He said to contact him before I write the following year's Chargers preview and he'll be happy to provide his insights. It can't hurt. So one more name has been added to my NFL rolodex.

INSIGHTS FROM THE REAL NFL DRAFT

I start getting really revved up again for football during the NFL draft, usually held in April. This is where NFL teams pick the best of the college crop and where trades often get consummated rather than just talked about. For fantasy football players, this is the most important football event of the year—not the Super Bowl. So make sure to watch, even if you're sick of listening to Chris Berman's shtick and looking at Mel Kiper's pompadour, because the information is good. Some of these guys know what they're talking about and are worth listening to.

At no other time of the year do so many sharp minds gather to talk about players and analyze teams. It's not just about the rookies. Each team is dissected and discussed by experts, coaches, players, and personnel department people. A lot can be learned. The main televised portion of the draft's first day goes seven hours. I find it the fastest seven hours in television. It's the NFL's version of political election coverage. So give up that one spring Saturday—this is fantasy football day.

If you can't watch the draft live, make sure to at least tape it. I've been closely following the NFL draft since the days George Allen was trading every Washington Redskins draft pick for grizzled veterans on social security. I've always been able to pick up, at the very least, several nuggets of good player information.

For instance, in the 2004 draft, when the Redskins, with the fifth pick, took safety Sean Taylor instead of tight end Kellen Winslow Jr., it was an indication Washington Coach Joe Gibbs cared more about adding to his defense than upgrading his passing attack. Sure enough, the Redskins finished twenty-ninth in passing yards.

Of the seven wide receivers taken in the first round of the 2004 draft, I thought Roy Williams had the best chance of making an impact his rookie year. My opinion was cemented watching the NFL draft when it was talked about how Williams may have been the top overall pick in the 2003 draft, but instead he went back to play for Texas his senior season instead of declaring for the draft early. Williams turned out be much more polished than normally expected for a rookie.

It's not just what is said during the draft, but also what is implied that is important. Sometimes you gain information by reading between the lines. You often get strong clues about teams and players. When the Rams traded up in the first round of the 2004 draft to take running back Steven Jackson, it validated a lot of opinions that Marshall Faulk was no longer worth taking in the first round of fantasy drafts.

In the 2001 draft, the Saints surprised people by taking Deuce McAllister with their number one pick, despite already having Ricky Williams. That's a red flag that the team had some doubts about Williams. Sure enough, the following year Williams was traded to the Dolphins. Two years later Williams quit the Dolphins, unexpectedly destroying their 2004 season. The draft gives you a window to peak inside a player with personality profile features and interviews. In the case of Williams, you could see he was a free spirit, marching to his own beat. That may be fine for artists, but not necessarily football players.

Be especially skeptical of rookie quarterbacks. Ben Roethlisberger had a dream season his rookie year for the Steelers. But his fantasy statistics were mediocre. Roethlisberger, though, was Johnny Unitas compared to Eli Manning, the top overall pick of the 2004 draft. Manning completed just 48 percent of his passes, had six touchdown passes and nine interceptions. He started the Giants final seven games and averaged 139 yards passing.

Bill Walsh once said, "More drafting mistakes are made on quarterbacks than at any other position." It took the Chargers eight years to recover from taking Ryan Leaf with the second overall pick in the 1998 draft. Leaf had the physical qualities to be a good quarterback, but he couldn't handle mental adversity. So no matter how much praise you hear about college quarterbacks, keep a cynical attitude. Don't just study their statistics. Get some idea of their mental makeup. Rookie running backs can make an impact right away whether they're head cases or not. Rookie quarterbacks rarely do.

NFL teams tear down and build much more rapidly now. They have to because of free-agency. The direction they go often becomes clearer during the draft. Usually a flurry of trades occurs. Things often move slowly in the NFL, especially during the off-season. That's not the case during the draft. Decisions get made then. Watching the draft not only keeps you up on the decisions, but presents a great opportunity to get some perspective on them.

The NFL draft signals your vacation from fantasy football is over. You've had two months away. Now it's time to begin preparing for the coming season. So don't just watch the NFL draft and then not read anything until August. The NFL is hot right after the draft. Interest is high. Newspapers and talk shows are full of NFL again. There is plenty of post-draft analysis to read. Stick closely with football during the week leading up to and following the NFL draft. It could pay off when you draft in the fall.

PROJECTIONS

Having a good draft is instrumental in fantasy football and the key to drafting good players is projecting. This is the skill of determining ahead of time which players will probably do well in the coming season and which won't. It's part science, part art, and to be honest, part luck.

The basis of your research involves statistics. Your starting point is looking at the player's numbers from last season. Some fantasy owners make the mistake of basing their draft just on the previous season's statistics. Treat those numbers as just a guide. There are no guarantees. Things change from season to season. The NFL ages like dog years—things evolve at a rapid pace. Running backs lose a step, kickers lose their confidence, wide receivers change systems, quarterbacks start hearing footsteps, defenses constantly break in new starters, and a team's chemistry comes and goes.

Inside the Numbers

The best fantasy owners look inside the numbers. They don't just take statistics at face value. Often there are reasons that account for a player's final figures. The Lions' Roy Williams, for instance, finished thirty-sixth in receiving yards and just out of the top forty in pass receptions in 2004. The Patriots' David Givens ranked ahead of Williams in both categories. Going solely by statistics, Williams would be ranked a "C" type receiver and Givens would be rated ahead of him.

In reality, Williams is a blossoming star, while Givens is just an interchangeable part of a crowed Patriots' receiving field. Williams was a rookie in 2004. He has a huge upside. He missed two games with a sprained ankle, and was hobbled in several others, which detracted from his final numbers. Williams faced a lot of double-teams because the Lions were without injured Charles Rogers, their other prize young wide receiver.

The Lions also didn't get stellar quarterback play from Joey Harrington. The Lions added Jeff Garcia to upgrade their quarterback position. Williams plays on carpet in a division with weak secondaries. These are all factors that help you make a projection on Williams. Hopefully you'll realize Williams is a "B" wide receiver and deserves to be ranked much higher than Givens despite that year's numbers. This is the type of scrutiny you need when making projections.

The secret is not just to crunch numbers but to analyze. Sure, you have to study numbers. I look at the player's entire career, checking to see if he's ever produced big figures. If he has, then he's proven capable. But what a player did five years ago has little relevancy to what he's going to do right now. If a player had a down season the year before, try to decipher why. Did he miss games? Was he playing hurt? Was he in a new system with different players? Did he lack motivation for one reason or another?

Consequently, if a player is coming off a good season, attempt to understand why. Was it a fluke, where circumstances came into play? Did he catch opponents by surprise? Did it happen to be his contract year? And, most important, is he capable of doing it again? This is where fantasy magazines can be a help, because projections are a big part of their preseason editorial content.

Breakout Players and Underachievers

Ideally in the later rounds you want to take players who can still improve. Often these are young players who have shown progress and potential and are ready for a breakout season. Green Bay wide receiver Javon Walker was such a player in 2004. He had looked great in training camp, was in his third season in the league all with the Packers, had a great quarterback in Brett Favre, was playing in a weak division, and opposing defenses were keying on running back Ahman Green.

Everything was in place and Walker came through, finishing third in receiving yards with 1,382 while scoring twelve touchdowns. The year before Walker had shown glimmers of his big-play potential averaging an NFC-high 17.5 yards per reception and hauling in nine touchdowns.

These are the type of situations and variables worth examining.

Unfortunately, it's easy to confuse a potential breakout player with a career underachiever. This is a category where guys like Donte Stallworth and Koren Robinson reside. They are high draft picks with tantalizing talent that never materializes except for brief, teasing glimpses. There are always excuses—injuries, and in the case of Robinson in 2004, a four-game league suspension. They might look great without pads in practice. They might even produce a big game or two, but they can't ever be trusted. Don't get caught overrating this type when doing projections.

Projecting Superstars

It's easier to project superstars. Everybody knows who they are. Sometimes, though, studs move to another team. The trick then is to gauge if their play will go up or down. A lot depends on how their new team uses them. After seven years with the Bengals, who never finished above .500 during that time, Corey Dillon was traded to the defending world champion Patriots in 2004. He responded with a career-high 1,635 yards rushing and twelve touchdowns. Dillon's previous bests were 1,435 yards rushing and ten touchdowns.

Clinton Portis, on the other hand, was traded away from a playoff team in Denver to a below .500 team in the Redskins. Portis's numbers shrunk from 1,591 yards rushing and fourteen touchdowns in 2003 to 1,315 yards rushing and just five touchdowns with the Redskins in

2004 despite fifty-three more rushing attempts. Some of this can be explained by Portis not being comfortable in a different offense, which was better suited for an inside power runner rather than a smallish-type back with breakaway speed and moves.

The Offensive System

It gets tricky making projections on wide receivers when they have a new quarterback. Often it's not good. For the first time in six years, Giants wide receiver Amani Toomer failed to get 1,000 yards receiving, finishing with just 747 yards in 2004. He also did not score after averaging five touchdowns the previous six seasons. A big reason for Toomer's decline was adjusting to two new quarterbacks, Kurt Warner and rookie Eli Manning. Hines Ward caught 80 passes for 1,004 yards and four touchdowns in 2004.

The previous two years, Ward averaged 103 receptions, 1,246 yards and eleven touchdowns. At twenty-eight, Ward still was at his peak. His production dwindled because the Steelers switched to a conservative, ground-oriented offense when rookie Ben Roethlisberger became the starting quarterback. So even though Ward's talent level hasn't dropped, you have to lower your expectations of him because the team has switched its offensive philosophy.

On ability alone I would rank Andre Johnson among the top five receivers. But when making projections, you have to take into account all factors. Johnson plays for the Texans. Their quarterback, David Carr, has not experienced a true breakout season. He has yet to throw for more than 3,600 yards and more than sixteen touchdown passes during his first three seasons in the league.

Texans Coach Dom Capers has not yet opened his offense to showcase Johnson. Maybe that will change in 2005. If you believe those factors will happen, then chances are you have high projections for Johnson.

The Big Picture

The bottom line is taking into account more than just numbers in establishing your projections. Take the total picture into consideration. If you're planning on grabbing a quarterback high in your draft, better make darn sure he's going to throw more than thirty touchdowns. It's not just talent with Peyton Manning. He has excellent receivers, plays his home games indoors in perfect weather conditions and has a top pass-blocking offensive line. He's in the optimum situation to succeed.

CHEAT SHEETS

Cheat sheets are the final player rankings and position lists you bring to the draft. All your work, preparation, and analysis should be summed up in these sheets. They are a shortcut on what players to take and when.

I've seen owners come to their draft with as little as one magazine, as well as owners who come loaded down like pack mules. Some even bring a laptop computer. That's fine—just make your sure your batteries aren't low, or the venue has convenient plug-in outlets. The important thing is to have some kind of guide to help you along whether it's on paper, newspaper, magazine, or computer.

One owner in our league comes to the draft with all the players written down on cardboard in big letters with each position marked in a different color. The owner doesn't wear glasses, but he doesn't want to take any chances. Even Mr. Magoo could see it.

Another owner uses a miniature draft board. Some like to bring a magazine and check off the names as they get picked. I don't like a lot of clutter, so all I take to my draft is two spiral notebooks. One is my cheat sheet listing the players and positions. My other spiral notebook is where I have each owner's name written down in order of where they'll be drafting. I use this notebook to write down each person's pick as soon as it happens.

The important thing about cheat sheets is finding the method that works for you. If you've done your homework and feel confident, then travel light. If you haven't had enough time to research, have a draft that goes a lot of rounds, and your league has many extra categories such as tackles, sacks, and interceptions, then bring as much reference material as needed. Don't get caught short. It's better to have too much data than not enough.

But be organized. If you have to bring a lot of notes, then know immediately where to turn to find your information. There's nothing worse than being on the clock and having no clue who you want to pick. Your final player determinations should come before, not during, your draft. Some owner's cheat sheets not only include a list of the best players at each position, but also a master sheet listing in descending order—from most valuable to least valuable—every player regardless of position.

I'll rate just the first fourteen players I would choose highest. That covers me through the first round. It's hard to map your draft beyond the first round, though. You should have an idea, or strategy, of who you want in the second, third, fourth, and fifth rounds. However, you can't realistically plan that far ahead because you never can be sure who your opponents will be selecting. It's a mistake to be too rigid.

Here's where your cheat sheets are crucial. Your player rankings, positions, and bye weeks are right in front of you. You can list them in tiers. That's the system I prefer. At each position I list the players as either "A," "B," "C," or "D." The "A" players are obviously the blue-chip top of the line. The "B" players are solid starters. The "C" ranking connotes borderline starters, while "D" players are fill-ins.

I'll also use plus and minus to break things down into sub-categories. For instance, I might rank Keyshawn Johnson a "B minus" wide receiver while listing David Givens as a "C plus." By looking at my cheat sheet, I'll know to take Johnson ahead of Givens if I need a receiver at that point in the draft. It's far easier to analyze and reach conclusions with these rankings than having to do it on the spur of the moment.

Just in case, I also compose an "F" list. These are players I'm not interested in, but file in a worst-case scenario. Again, you don't want to be caught out of players to choose from with one or two rounds left. That includes reserves who, with luck or injuries to starters, could turn into first-stringers. That's why a contingency list or "F" category is necessary.

The chart on the next page shows my spring 2005 quarterback cheat sheet.

By my rankings, I would be safe getting at least a "B" quarterback in a fourteen-owner league since I rated fourteen quarterbacks with a "B" grade or higher. I never want to sink past a "B" ranking in taking a starting quarterback. If I couldn't land any of my three "A" quarterbacks—Manning, Culpepper, or McNabb—I wouldn't be in a big hurry to take my starting quarterback since I consider the next eleven quarterbacks around even. I might favor Green slightly more than Brees, but I'd rather take Brees in the sixth round than Green in the third round.

There are many styles of working from cheat sheets. Some owners rank players from top to bottom and just keep choosing the highest-rated player left when it's their turn. Many basic online leagues operate this way. You pre-rank each player and the computer drafts your team going from one position to the next. The danger in that method is ending up with an unbalanced roster, where you might have three excellent quarterbacks and two outstanding kickers, but not be strong at a key spot like running back or wide receiver.

SPRING 2005 QUARTERBACK CHEAT SHEET

A-Plus	**C-Minus**
Peyton Manning	Drew Bledsoe
Daunte Culpepper	Kyle Boller
	Eli Manning
A-Minus	Brian Griese
Donovan McNabb	Rex Grossman
B	**D**
Trent Green	Patrick Ramsey
Michael Vick	J.P. Losman
Jake Plummer	Trent Dilfer
Brett Favre	Alex Smith
Tom Brady	A.J. Feeley
Kerry Collins	Joey Harrington
Matt Hasselbeck	Tim Rattay
Chad Pennington	Billy Volek
Marc Bulger	
Aaron Brooks	**F**
	Gus Frerotte
B-Minus	Brad Johnson
Drew Brees	Kelly Holcomb
	Chris Simms
C-Plus	Jason Campbell
Jake Delhomme	Matt Schaub
Steve McNair	Drew Henson
Carson Palmer	Philip Rivers
	Josh McCown
C	Charlie Frye
David Carr	
Jeff Garcia	
Kurt Warner	
Byron Leftwich	
Ben Roethlisberger	

PREPARING FOR YOUR SEASON

The Dangers of Using Certain Sources

Fantasy football magazines are chock full of cheat sheets. Some owners just use those magazine rankings as their draft guide. I would caution against that. Magazine deadlines are well in advance of when the publication comes out and changes occur daily in the NFL. Those writing for magazines and Web sites might be referred to as experts, but their rankings aren't necessarily any better than yours. Don't be unduly influenced to take a certain player just because some magazine writer lauds that player two months before your draft.

Michael Vick is a popular cover choice for magazines. He often is listed high in cheat sheets. But since becoming a starter in 2002, Vick has never finished better than eighteenth in passing yards or thrown for more than 16 touchdowns in a season going into 2005. Vick is a great athlete and runner, but from a passing standpoint, it has been a mistake to rank him so high in cheat sheets.

Magazines and Web sites help create public perception when they run cheat sheets. But you have to take into account your league structure and fellow owners before making any final player determinations. Frank Sanders, for instance, turned out to be a great pick in 1998 for those in leagues where receptions counted. Sanders led the NFC with eighty-nine catches that season, but he scored only three touchdowns. So in touchdown-dominated leagues, Sanders would rate a lot lower.

Cheat Sheet Summary

The key is to be flexible. Rarely, though, will you be able to have a perfect draft where everything falls neatly into place. If you're already loaded at a position and the next highest player you have ranked plays that same position, you need to see how big of a drop there is to take a player at another position. That's where your cheat sheet comes in most handy. Your cheat sheet is your playbook. Cling to it.

BYE WEEKS

Bye weeks can't be avoided. At some point in the season, each team is going to have a week off from playing. That's mandated by the NFL. Byes have been a part of the NFL fabric since 1990, and they're not going away. If anything, I wouldn't be shocked if some time down the road the NFL adds a second bye week, stretching the season even more.

Bye weeks can be annoying because any of your players on a team that is idle that week obviously can't score any points for you. Look on the bright side of byes—you don't lose any points, and your players get an extra week to heal from their injuries. Plus, byes add strategy, and anything that adds extra strategy to fantasy football is better for the sharper owner.

You know each NFL team is going to be off one week at some point during the season, so it's imperative to know exactly when each team's bye occurs when drafting and making out your lineup because you need to have replacements for any starting player off because of a bye.

PREPARING FOR YOUR SEASON

Planning ahead separates the sophisticated owner from the amateur.

I'm not one for a lot of paper clutter during the draft. It's always amusing and empowering to see owners frantically flip through their magazines and massive notes in search of their next draft pick, all the while pathetically pleading for more time. But one essential item you do need in front of you is a list showing the bye weeks. Even if you have the bye weeks memorized, still keep this information handy. So much goes on during the draft that your mind can develop brain lock. You need precise information. You can't be guessing if the Bills are off in Week 3 or Week 4.

Some leagues require multiple quarterbacks and kickers in your lineup. It's a bad mistake to end up with both your kickers and quarterbacks off the same week. Some leagues also require a tight end. I don't advocate drafting more than one tight end because their input can be minimal if you don't have a good one. Tight end is the one spot I don't replace when my tight end has his bye, unless a better tight end happens to be in the free agent pool or waivers. It's not worth the extra dollars you have to pay in transaction fees.

Some leagues also restrict the number of moves you can make each week. If, say, you're limited to two moves each week, there's a chance you'll need to address more serious areas during bye weeks than fishing for a tight end in a pool of part-timers and blocking specialists. If you have room on your bench, and don't mind paying the transaction fee, than go ahead and pick up a tight end for that week. Just don't be shocked if he fails to score any points for you.

Drafting Brett Favre in one head-to-head league during 2004, I gambled by not taking a backup quarterback, knowing Favre is indestructible and wouldn't have his bye until Week 9. By doing this, I added flexibility to either stash another running back, or have a bigger selection of wide receivers to choose from on my bench. Eventually I picked up my backup quarterback, Brian Griese, in Week 6. So for five weeks I enjoyed a free ride at quarterback without a backup. Do not, however, attempt this strategy with a fragile quarterback, like, for example, Steve McNair. The key here is making sure there are still a few starting quarterbacks left in the free agent pool. Remember, I just needed a quarterback for the one week Favre was idle.

Projecting Value

You need to be up on byes two to three weeks in advance. Because the NFL landscape changes from week to week, sometimes drastically, it doesn't really pay to project value earlier than two to three weeks down the road. I had the Patriots defense in my head-to-head league in 2004. Knowing the Patriots' bye was in Week 3, I also took the Raiders defense late during the draft. The Raiders were hosting the Buccaneers in Week 3 and the Bucs offense was not looking good at the time. So I was projecting what defense would be solid just for that Week 3. Sure enough, the Raiders defense scored double-digit points for me, helping me win that week despite being without my number one defense.

If the Patriots would have had a much later bye, there would have been no urgency to take a second defense in the draft. I simply would have waited until a couple of weeks before New England's bye, and then tried to figure out which defense in the free agent pool would be the most effective for the particular week I would need them. The trick here is making sure there still are enough choices in the free agent pool. You never want to be caught short.

Always Take Quality

It's not worth it to pass on a good running back or wide receiver during the draft if their bye week happens to fall the same date as your other starters. You should have enough depth at those key positions, especially wide receiver. It's better in the long run to have upgraded quality at these spots than to take a lesser player just to avoid a bye conflict. Plus, in most leagues you can make trades. Don't ever cut a decent player just because it's his bye week. Pick up a temporary replacement from the free agent pool. It's only for one week, and you might just get lucky short-term with that player.

Preparation is Key

Above all, don't let a bye week catch you by surprise. Be up on them in advance. Plan ahead.

STRENGTH OF SCHEDULE

As part of your draft preparation you want to examine the difficulty of each team's schedule. Just because a team's schedule looks hard in July doesn't mean it will stay that way in November.

In the free-agency, parity-driven NFL the last can become first and the first become last. The Oakland Raiders proved that in 2003 finishing 4-12 after reaching the Super Bowl the previous season. The Giants finished under .500 in 2001 after making the Super Bowl in 2000. The Carolina Panthers reached the Super Bowl in 2003 and finished under .500 the following season. A sudden retirement, like what happened to the Dolphins with Ricky Williams before the 2004 season, or a key preseason injury, like what happened to Michael Vick in 2003, can devastate a team and throw things out of whack.

The NFL tabulates each team's won-lost records in coming up with its strength-of-schedule rankings. They don't factor in statistics. That skews things from a fantasy perspective because it doesn't take into account teams that had bad defenses but still managed a good won-lost mark. The Chiefs, for instance, were 13-3 in 2003. Yet they had the twenty-ninth-ranked defense. So it was a positive, not a negative, to have your fantasy players go against the Chiefs in 2004. The Chiefs ended up finishing thirty-first in team defense in 2004.

The Jets played one of the most difficult schedules in 2004, but Curtis Martin still managed to lead the NFL in rushing. He did this by going against six of the top-ranked defenses by the previous season's standards during the first nine games. On the other hand, the Falcons, Seahawks, Cardinals, and Bears had four of the easiest schedules during 2004. But their quarterbacks fared poorly. Of the four teams' quarterbacks, the Seahawks' Matt Hasselbeck placed the highest, finishing fourteenth in passing yards and seventeenth in quarterback rating. Vick finished twenty-first in quarterback rating and the Cardinals' Josh McCown ranked twenty-ninth. The Bears quarterbacks were so miserable they ranked off the charts.

This isn't to say you should ignore strength of schedule. It can be a useful tool. I ranked Daunte Culpepper the number two quarterback going into 2004 behind only Peyton Manning. One factor for Culpepper's high ranking was his Vikings had seven games against teams whose pass defense ranked twenty-fifth or worse. Culpepper put up a monster season, leading the NFL in passing yards while throwing for 39 touchdowns.

Jake Plummer and Jake Delhomme had career seasons, too, in 2004 for the Broncos and Panthers, respectively. Plummer got to throw four times against the thirty-first and thirtieth defensive-ranked Chiefs and Raiders, while Delhomme faced a number of terrible secondaries, including the Saints twice, Packers, Chiefs, Raiders, and 49ers.

On the flip side, I downgraded the Redskins' Clinton Portis, because, based on strength-of-schedule ratings, he and the Redskins would be facing the league's toughest run defense. Sure enough, Portis scored just five touchdowns after scoring a combined 29 his first two years with the Broncos. He averaged 3.8 yards a carry, where in the previous two seasons he averaged 5.5 yards per attempt.

So while it's certainly not foolproof, studying a team's schedule can prove beneficial to your results. However, you don't want to pass on a star player no matter how daunting his team's schedule appears. Peyton Manning is going to put up big numbers regardless of who he's playing, except maybe against Bill Belichick's Patriots on a cold, winter day in Foxboro.

Strength of schedule should only account for about 10 percent of a player's value. It mainly comes in handy as a deciding factor when trying to determine who to rank higher between two players of seemingly equal value.

Make Your Own Ratings

For strength of schedule to have fantasy significance you need to break it down by team statistics, not won-lost record. You'll get a more accurate strength of schedule reading if you tweak the ratings to fit for fantasy purposes rather than by won-lost records. Try doing your own strength of schedule rankings. Don't go strictly by won-lost records. The Colts went 12-4 in 2004, but finished twenty-ninth in defense. They gave up the sixth-most touchdown passes and were twenty-fourth in rushing defense. Those should be your numbers in shaping your strength of schedule power ratings for the Colts, not their fancy won-lost mark.

The Dolphins, on the other hand, went 4-12 but were eighth in defense. The Cardinals finished 6-10 in the weak NFC West, but were ninth in pass defense and thirteenth in fewest rushing touchdowns allowed. So their defense was more competitive than their won-lost record might have indicated.

An Example from 2004 and 2005

A lot changes during the off-season when teams lose players and sign free agents. This isn't factored when strength of schedule information is released. You just can't pencil in a player's projected stats for the coming season based on last year. The Bengals and Jets, for instance, played difficult schedules in 2004. But in 2005, the schedule lightened up considerably for them.

Going into the 2005 season, this is how I looked at things: The Bengals got the NFC North teams. That was a huge plus for Cincinnati quarterback Carson Palmer. He got to throw against the Packers, who gave up a franchise-worst 33 touchdown passes in 2004; the Vikings, who finished twenty-ninth in pass defense; and the Lions, who were twenty-first in pass defense and allowed the sixth-most touchdown passes.

Jets quarterback Chad Pennington got to operate against the defensively-challenged AFC West teams. The Chiefs, Chargers, Raiders, and Saints all ranked among the six-worst pass defenses in 2004. Never mind the Chargers went 12-4 in 2004. For fantasy purposes, what matters most in assessing strength of schedule is that they ranked thirtieth in pass defense. Their rush defense, though, was rated number three, which was good news for Pennington and his wide receivers.

MOCK DRAFTS

A **mock draft** is a practice draft. Mock drafts have become so popular that there are specific interactive Web sites, such as MockDraftCentral.com, specializing in conducting them. There is also software available to help you set them up yourself. Mock drafts can be organized and run on fantasy football message boards, too. They have been an underutilized tool so far, but more owners are starting to realize the benefits of them. It's worth doing at least one mock draft just for the practice, especially if you know your draft position in advance.

If you don't know your position, then try picking at the top, middle, or end spots. Chances are you'll get a vastly different flavor of the draft. It makes sense that the more you practice something, the better you should be.

At a mock draft, it isn't necessarily your goal to see which players might be available in the first round, since it's essentially a given who the top players selected will be. Instead, use the mock draft to try to find out who could be available in the ensuing rounds. While the top runners are often grouped together, there's a much bigger difference of opinion on and wider gap between the best wide receivers once you get past Randy Moss, Terrell Owens, and Marvin Harrison.

A mock draft enables you to work out some twists in your drafting, hopefully get any mistakes out of your system, and get a better feel on when to take a certain player. You can see when position runs might occur, when the first kicker gets taken, and how soon a run on tight ends might happen. You'll be able to have a better idea on how long you can wait before taking players you've been targeting.

After doing several mock drafts, you will have a lower chance of getting blindsided on certain players and positions. You'll have an idea of the timing and what other owners are thinking. Sure, there is probably at least one owner in your league who is famous for throwing curveballs on his selections. But at least by doing one trial run you'll be better equipped to deal with any contingencies or surprises that often come up in drafts.

You've probably kicked yourself too many times for allowing a player you really wanted to slip by because you waited too long. I know I have. There have also been times where I've wondered if I took a player too soon. It is embarrassing to draft a player and then six rounds later hear some other owner ask if that player is available. Mock drafts give you a feel·for all that. They are the equivalent of playing preseason games.

Test Your Strategy

Besides getting the kinks out, mock drafts are good for trying out various strategies. You have nothing to lose, since these drafts don't count. So test how your team would look if you don't take a running back in the first three rounds, or try the opposite approach by taking three stud runners with your first three picks. See what good players still would be left in the fourth and fifth rounds if you pick up a tight end in the third round. Find out how long it takes before the last quality quarterback gets drafted. Test to see if you can get away with taking a defense or kicker before anyone else.

Every year there are players who are wild cards because no one can say with any degree of accuracy where they will be drafted. Thomas Jones was such a player going into 2004. In mock drafts conducted in June he was going in the middle rounds. But by the time of the final mock drafts in early September, right before the season kicked off, Jones was targeted by some owners as an early second-round pick as more information came out about how the Bears were going to feature him as the centerpiece of their offense. Wide receivers are a better example of typical wild cards because there are so many good ones. I especially like Andre Johnson. Will I be able to get him in the fourth round, or is that too late? Mock drafts can help answer questions like that.

Domanick Davis and Javon Walker are two prime examples from 2004. Because of mock drafts and the publicity surrounding them, it was determined that if you wanted Davis, you couldn't wait past the middle of the second round. Walker moved up the charts fast in mock drafts, too. Those participating in mock drafts realized that if they wanted Walker, they probably would have to take him a round sooner than was originally expected. I'm sure there were some surprised owners in a few leagues when Walker went in the middle rounds during many 2004 drafts. They probably wouldn't have been if they had done a couple of mock drafts.

This isn't your real draft, so there's no reason to get mad if you miss out on a player or make a questionable choice. The objective with mock drafts isn't to come away with the all-perfect team. Does anyone remember who won during preseason? No, and who cares? It's the same theory with mock drafts. Their major purpose is to help you learn and analyze not just your selections, but the entire board. Ask yourself, what were some of the surprises? What did you do well? What did you do poorly? And most importantly: What did you learn that can make your draft better the next time?

Public Perception

During the months leading up to opening week, various publications come out with how their so-called experts did in mock drafts. This can be helpful, but can also influence some fantasy football participants to overrate or underrate certain players. One supposed expert picked Domanick Davis in the first round in every mock draft he participated in during 2004. That publicity certainly didn't hurt Davis's draft status. While you might not agree with the assessment of these self-proclaimed experts, be aware that public perception can be influenced by them, since more and more people are buying fantasy football magazines and online premium services.

More Mock Draft Strategies

What you don't want to do is tip your hand when participating in a mock draft. So I'd advise doing them anonymously. You don't want your fellow league owners having any clue which players you're high on, who you're downgrading, and what strategy you might be experimenting with.

After doing a mock draft, try to communicate on a message board with the other participating owners about why they took certain players at certain spots. This isn't about criticism or making fun of someone's picks. It's about learning, being open-minded, and seeing if anyone has any opinions worth incorporating.

Be fair, though. Make it a two-way street. If other owners are honest and provide good information, then try to contribute likewise. I took Saints tight end Boo Williams in the tenth round of a mock draft in 2004. I wasn't sure if that was too high to pick him. So I asked for feedback and I received several informative messages. In return, I offered to analyze some of their picks. It doesn't hurt to solicit objective opinions following your mock draft.

Some fantasy football fanatics do ten to fifteen mock drafts. That's crazy. Doing a couple and studying other mock drafts are enough for me. You don't want to get burned out before the season even begins. For me, fantasy football begins in the spring with the NFL college player draft. Basically, it's a ten-month hobby, depending on your level of commitment.

SELECTING A DRAFT VENUE

Fantasy football is becoming so popular you need to reserve your draft venue weeks ahead, if not months, especially if you want to hold the draft right before the season kicks off. It's the same with online leagues. With all the millions of people competing, the premium dates—those days right before the season begins—are filled almost immediately on some of the popular free sites like Yahoo and ESPN. Don't be afraid to set up your draft early if your league and owners are all in place. If you're competing on the popular online sites, make sure to register early.

Face-to-Face Draft

Where is the best place to have your draft? I've drafted in a bar, restaurant, home, hotel, banquet room, business office, by phone, computer, and even at a public library. The easy answer is where you and your league feel most comfortable. The more realistic answer is wherever you can secure a big enough room.

My preference is a spacious, private area inside a bar or restaurant. If some out-of-town owner can't make it in person, a speaker phone with a suitable extension cord needs to be available. This way you can place the speaker phone in the middle of the room, so everyone can hear the picks and no one is at a disadvantage.

It's a good idea to visit the selected site before draft day. That way you can get a feel for the place and double-check the phone line. We still kid one of our out-of-town owners about the time the phone line didn't work at the tavern where we were holding our draft. This forced us to recruit a patron at the bar to draft for the out-of-town owner. The barfly said he knew football, but maybe that was just the beer talking, because in between belches he forgot to pick a starting quarterback, kicker, and number three wide receiver. He did have plenty of tight ends and backup quarterbacks, though.

You want your draft to be in a fun setting. There's nothing worse than practically having to whisper your picks. In the first year of my face-to-face league, we actually conducted our draft in a room at the public library. It felt weird having to act so serious about something that we were doing for entertainment.

At least everybody knew where the library was. One year we had an owner miss a draft because he couldn't find the venue. You don't want to pick a place that is off the beaten track. It's also a good idea to start on time, preferably with everyone present. Most of our owners enjoy getting to the draft early to eat and socialize since this is the only time some of us see each other. It's a good public relations gesture to greet and talk with everyone. It might come in handy some time when you're looking to make a trade.

Be careful when lining up your venue. I heard one horror story about a league that arranged to hold their draft at an upscale restaurant. However, when the appointed day and time came, they couldn't get the banquet room they had been promised. It turned out that another league had slipped the owner some money to give them the banquet room that day for their draft.

Most bars won't charge for a room. In turn, though, you need to give them enough food and beverage business to make it worth their while. It's only fair. This shouldn't be a difficult task for leagues with anywhere from ten to twenty people showing up, especially if there are some heavy drinkers. I still remember one Sunday morning draft where an owner celebrated his selection of Shaun Alexander by ordering a shot of Jagermeister to wash down his toast and scrambled eggs.

More bar owners are realizing that catering to fantasy football league drafts is a smart way to attract additional business. The owner of a bar and restaurant in Las Vegas is in several fantasy football leagues, and has set up a computer software system to handle all the teams that draft at his place. He makes a computer printout of everybody's picks. The only problem with his setup is the draft room is located next to the bar in an open space. With no doors, this can lead to distractions. Sure enough, when we conducted our draft at this establishment there was the obligatory drunk and his girlfriend at the bar screaming and shouting obscenities while watching a NASCAR event. It got so loud that we couldn't hear people's picks because the draft room was in an open area. Luckily the owner was there and handled the situation. The draft is the most fun day of the year. You don't want idiots ruining it.

The classiest place I ever drafted was in a banquet room at The Mirage hotel on the Las Vegas Strip. One of our league members at the time had juice there. It never hurts to see if any of your league members has an in at a choice spot. This is the time to call in a favor. Just make sure the place has a bathroom close by.

Online Draft

You don't have to worry about the logistics of finding a good location when doing an online league draft. Just make sure your computer is working and the family knows you absolutely can't be disturbed during that time. Have your draft lists and information sheets close by, because some online live drafts go extremely fast. This happens when owners can't be there and there is a one-minute time limit. The absent owners set up their draft lists and go on auto-pilot where the computer drafts for them using their prearranged draft order lists.

Many who participate in fantasy football online use an automated draft. This is where the league's computer program picks the team for you based on customized ratings you set up in advance. The computer will automatically draft your players from default rankings if you didn't have time to set up your own ratings.

Electing a Commissioner
Every league needs a commissioner, or at least a ruling body. Somebody has to make the final decisions on league matters and keep things organized. You can't have chaos and confusion if you want your league to work. Usually someone either volunteers for the commissioner position or is pushed into it. That's fine as long as the person is accepted by the majority. The commissioner should have the respect of his fellow league members. It is imperative that the commissioner be fair, honest, and objective. This isn't as easy as it may sound, because in almost all cases the commissioner has his own team in the league. So he's really under the microscope. One league I knew of nearly folded because its commissioner wasn't trusted by many of the owners.

If no one suitable volunteers, than the league can choose to be run by a three-or-five member committee. You need an odd number in order to break any voting ties. Another way to get a commissioner is for league members to entice someone to run by offering an incentive, like a free entry into the league.

The commissioner often serves as the treasurer, too, collecting and holding the money until the end of the season. These jobs can easily be handled by two different people. The benefit to being the treasurer is that you can make a little money on interest by depositing the funds in a bank for safekeeping.

Commissioners Before the Internet

In the old days—before the rise of the Internet—it was up to the commissioner or league secretary to add up, keep track of, and distribute statistics and standings. It was not a fun task, being nearly a full-time job in itself.

The first commissioner of our Las Vegas Low Rollers league did all the statistical work himself. This was in the mid-1990s. In the beginning it was a labor of love, but it got tough year after year for him. He finally relinquished his commissioner duties when he decided to switch careers and go to law school. Becoming a lawyer was less time consuming than running a fantasy football league, he said

Thankfully, things are one hundred times easier now because of the Internet. There are fantasy football Web sites, some of which are free, that can run your league and take care of statistics, transactions, and standings, all while serving as arbiter in case someone wants to protest a trade. But you still need someone to at least organize the league. That means inviting people to play, deciding if you want to have a private or public league, and choosing a stat company and Web site.

Commissioner Styles

I've played in fantasy leagues that have had all types of commissioners. One commissioner's approach was completely hands-off, letting just about any trade go through. His attitude about a lopsided deal was, "If you can screw someone, then good for you." I also played for many years with a commissioner who was completely the opposite. He monitored everything closely and was way too overprotective. He got upset and issued warnings to owners for not making enough moves. If an owner was sloppy running his team, not sending his moves in the correct way, this commissioner would kick him out. This guy made Judge Judy look like Shirley Temple.

I think the ideal commissioner style should be somewhere in the middle between these two. The commissioner needs to be flexible but firm. He has to be organized, understanding, and tactful in the manner he communicates and runs things. He should thoroughly know the rules. You don't want a shoddy league. Sometimes the hammer needs to be dropped on an owner. On the other hand, you don't want someone micromanaging the entire league. It's a tough balancing act. But it's worth the effort to find the right person for the position.

6. DRAFT AND AUCTION STRATEGIES

DRAFT STRATEGY

The draft is the highlight of the season when everyone comes together to select their players. Unlike the real NFL draft, fantasy drafts are done in **serpentine** fashion. That is, the team that has the last pick in the first round gets to make the opening pick of the second round, while the team picking first won't get its next selection until all the other owners have made their second round pick.

In a twelve owner draft, for instance, Team 12 would pick last in the first round and first in the second round. Then comes Team 11 with the second pick of the second round. Team 1's second-round pick wouldn't be chosen again until the twenty-fourth pick. Team 1 then opens the third round pick, followed by the team that had the second overall pick and so on. In other words, the draft is held in reverse order for even-numbered rounds. This makes things more balanced and fair.

Imagine it is draft day. The beer is on the table. Your notebooks are in proper position and your pen is poised. It's time to draft! Okay, so now what do you do? Be flexible. That's the key. If your pick is among the top

CARDOZA PUBLISHING • STEPHEN NOVER

eight, your choice is rather simple. It's either running back or quarterback. It's a case of supply and demand. Everybody needs at least two good running backs. There are not enough of them to go around. You want to get the most productive players you can. Usually that means a running back or quarterback. Here's how your overall strategy for the draft might look:

First Round

Unless you project a quarterback like Peyton Manning to throw 49 touchdown passes like he did in 2004, or Daunte Culpepper to pass and run for a combined 41 scores, you need to go running back. There usually are enough franchise backs to fill out the top eight spots. Priest Holmes, LaDainian Tomlinson, Ahman Green, Clinton Portis, Shaun Alexander, Deuce McAllister, Edgerrin James, and Jamal Lewis were scooped up as the top eight picks in many 2004 drafts.

If you're picking in the nine to twelve range of the first round, your options are to take one of the three highest-rated quarterbacks, go with a lesser but very solid running back like a Fred Taylor, or take the premier wide receiver. The important thing is to have some idea of which way you want to go in the second round. Your pick is going to come up very soon again in typical drafts that use the **serpentine method,** also called a **snake rotation,** where whoever picks first doesn't pick again until everyone has made two selections, as described earlier.

Those picking high in the draft don't have that luxury. They can't say for sure which players are going to be there when the draft comes all the way around to their turn again.

Second Round

You need to seriously consider a running back in the second round if you didn't take one in the opening round. The negative aspect of taking a quarterback with a top-five pick in twelve-team leagues is that by the time your choice comes back to you, there could be seventeen to eighteen running backs off the board. I've been involved in drafts where the first fifteen picks were all running backs.

Those picking early in the second round should have their choice of the "B" running backs, upper tier quarterbacks, and "A" wide receivers. It's tempting to take a dominant wide receiver like a Randy Moss or Terrell Owens if they are available here. Most likely I'd go that direction, or take a reliable running back rather than choose a quarterback. Not only do quarterbacks get hurt frequently, but there is a lot of depth at the position. Teams need just one quarterback. But they need two running backs. That thins out the position.

I drew the twelfth pick out of fourteen in a mock draft held two months prior to the 2004 season. My first three picks were running backs—Rudi Johnson, Fred Taylor, and Thomas Jones. I was still able to get Chad Pennington in the middle rounds, and was also able to land several good receivers, including Isaac Bruce, Eric Moulds, and Donald Driver.

Third Round

Yes, it's nice to have Manning or Culpepper as your triggerman. But if you can't get them, don't be in a rush to find your quarterback. There are enough good ones to go around. If there's still a dominant quarterback available like Michael Vick or Donovan McNabb, he could make a worthy third-round pick.

If you've gone running back/running back with your first two picks you would be justified in gobbling up any elite quarterback or wide receiver if one is still available. Flexibility is huge in this round. There's no law that says you can't take another running back, even if you've already taken them in the first and second rounds. I did it in the mock draft, but only because I was high on Thomas Jones. However, don't take a third running back on your third-round pick unless you believe he's going to have a big year.

A tough decision you may have to make in round three is whether to dip down to a "C" running back, or take a "B" wide receiver. If I already had one running back, and my "C" list of running backs was fairly extensive, I would take the better player, which would be the wide receiver in this case. I faced this situation in one of my 2004 leagues, opting to take Lee Suggs when I could have selected Joe Horn, Andre Johnson, or Darrell Jackson, all of whom were still available.

I wish I could have redone the pick. It turned out to be a mistake because Suggs couldn't stay healthy. You don't want to gamble during round three. If outstanding players are still in abundance, you don't need to take someone that high who has any kind of risk factor, such as a history of injuries.

Your top three players need to be safe, productive players you can count on each week. Don't draft players based solely on statistics from previous seasons. A player's value can go up or down based on many circumstances, like switching teams, being in a contract year, changing offensive systems, having new teammates, switching coaches, or coming back from an injury.

Fourth Round

If any high "B" player still is hanging around, round four is the time to pounce on him regardless of position. The exception would be if an upper tier quarterback is still there and you already have one. Unless you're in a league that starts two quarterbacks, you'll want to skip the quarterback and go running back or wide receiver. If you have just one running back, this is a round to seriously consider getting your other starting running back. The top two tight ends could figure here, too. Tony Gonzalez has been the number one rated tight end the past few years, usually going in the third round. I think that's a round too early, but I'd consider him with a late pick in the third round.

The fourth round is also a perfect round to get a solid, number two wide receiver. In many leagues, the fourth round is to wide receivers what the first round is to running backs. Everybody grabs a wide receiver. You would be doing very well if, at this stage of the draft, your lineup looked like this:

Round One: elite running back
Round Two: another outstanding running back or elite wide receiver
Round Three: upper tier quarterback, wide receiver, or solid running back
Round Four: "B" wide receiver

Fifth Round

The flavor of your draft should become clear by round five. Did a lot of running backs go as expected? Has there been a run on wide receivers? How many quality quarterbacks are still available? By now you should have running backs and at least one wide receiver. If you don't have a wide receiver, you need to take the best one available right away.

It's in round five where owners start to veer off in different directions. Some reach for a running back while others make their move on a quarterback. Some owners decide this is the time to grab a top-five rated tight end, and a few decide the wisest course is to take another good wide receiver. You need to check your cheat sheets and notes to see if you can still wait another round or two on a quarterback, if there are any worthy running backs left at this stage, and how deep the wide receiving crop is until you're dipping to a lower level.

The key is to get value in this round. There is no value taking a tight end unless he happens to be an "A" player. I don't usually want to grab my quarterback here if there are still enough good ones left on the board. I also don't want to reach for a mediocre running back just to have another runner if there are still undrafted "B" wide receivers. This is the round where you can follow that old axiom of best athlete available, or in fantasy terms, best skill position player still available.

Sixth Through Eighth Rounds

By the time you reach rounds six to eight you should have your running back and wide receiver starters in place. If some really outstanding player has managed to slip this far, this is the time to pluck him. This also is the area where you want to take your quarterback if you haven't landed one yet. It's amazing how many good quarterbacks are still available in these middle rounds.

I rate each player, assigning a grade from A to F. The secret to these middle rounds is checking your list to make sure you can still get "B" and high "C" players, rather than having to drop to the next tier. For example, in my 2004 draft league I had the last pick of the third round. I had gone wide receiver (Randy Moss), running back (the regrettable Kevan Barlow) on my first two picks. I anticipated going running back or wide receiver, but Donovan McNabb was still available. He was the last "A" quarterback on my list. There would be a drop in the quarterback level after McNabb. So I switched gears and made McNabb my third-round pick. It's crucial to keep an open mind in the middle rounds.

Round eight isn't a bad spot to take a shot on a running back that has been downgraded for any number of reasons, but still has a huge upside. This might be a player coming off an injury, an underachiever, a promising backup who might finally be in line for an increased role, a player on a new team competing to be the featured back, or an aging veteran who always seems to be good for touchdowns. What you want here is a running back who can potentially transform your team. Sure, there are going to be flaws. That's why the running back lasted this long. But if he hits, you've picked up a winner at a small price.

Ninth Through Eleventh Rounds

Some owners take their kicker and defense during rounds nine to eleven. That's too soon. Kickers are just too unreliable. Kicking leaders change from season to season. You certainly factor strong offenses and weather conditions in evaluating kickers, but there is still no way you can accurately determine which ones will get the most field goal opportunities. It's just too random a position. One year Martin Gramatica was a top-ten kicker; the following year he lost his job.

I would be more tempted to take a defense in round eleven, but only one ranked among the top three. There's no rush in that area, either. Defenses can turn sour in a short time because of free agency, cluster injury problems, and offenses learning how to attack them after an offseason of preparation. The Panthers, for instance, ranked number two in defense in 2002 so they were taken high in 2003 drafts. But that season they dropped to eighth, and in 2004 their defense plummeted all the way to twentieth.

DRAFT AND AUCTION STRATEGIES

I'd rather take a good tight end, back up my quarterback and wide receiver spots, and shore up my running back depth in rounds nine to eleven. If you missed out on getting an "A" or "B" quarterback, you can fall back on a quarterback by committee strategy. These are the rounds to draft your quarterbacks if adopting that strategy. You need to land two quarterbacks, if not three, from the "C" tier. That way you'll have better options at the position each week depending on the various matchups. You can't wait any longer, however, if you don't have your triggerman. You don't want to be left with just debris and dreck to choose from.

Twelfth Through Fourteenth Rounds

By rounds twelve to fourteen some owners have lost their intensity and are reduced to just throwing darts. Don't get caught up in that. Keep your focus and concentration. There's still a lot of work and strategy left. A top-ten defense might be of interest here. So would another wide receiver. There should be many starting wide receivers still on the board. Some lucky owners in 2004 were able to get Muhsin Muhammad, Drew Bennett, and Brandon Stokley this late. This is the time to **handcuff;** that is, draft the backup on the same team as your key starters. This means taking the Titans' Billy Volek at quarterback if you've already taken injury-prone Steve McNair. In the case of running backs it means drafting the Chargers' or Chiefs' top backup running back if you have LaDainian Tomlinson or Priest Holmes. This proved to be sound strategy for those who drafted both

Kurt Warner and Marc Bulger in 2003. There's no way of predicting injuries, but this way you can protect yourself. It's like buying insurance.

Sometimes you can strike gold in these late rounds by taking reserves from powerful offenses such as drafting the Colts' number three wide receiver, which happened to be Stokley in 2004, or a talented running back in a crowded backfield-type situation such as the Vikings' Mewelde Moore. This is being proactive, where you're only risking a late pick on a situation that, if it breaks your way, could pay huge dividends.

Fifteenth Through Seventeenth Rounds
The final two to three rounds of your draft is when you can fill out your roster with a kicker, defense, and tight end, while making sure you have adequate backups. It's okay to take a flyer on certain players, such as a quality backup quarterback like a Kelly Holcomb, Jon Kitna, and Tommy Maddox, knowing they can put up solid numbers if given the opportunity, or a backup quarterback from an outstanding offense.

Chances are that quarterback—such as the backup for the Colts, Packers, Chiefs, and Patriots—won't ever see the field. But if he does, you could be in business. This is what happened with Bulger and the Rams when Warner got hurt. Bulger put up monster numbers running the Rams' high-powered attack. Remember, Warner came to prominence when then-Rams starter Trent Green was knocked out for the season during a 2001 preseason game.

Keep paying attention. You never know when an opportunity might pop up during the draft. It's what you prepared for all year.

AUCTION STRATEGY

The popularity of acquiring your players through an auction is on the rise. In this format, league owners take turns bringing up different players' names for bid. An auctioneer, who can be a fellow league owner, is necessary to organize and speed along the bidding process. It's more democratic when everyone has a chance to get whomever they desire. That doesn't happen in a draft league. I know I've felt frustrated sitting hopelessly by during a draft, waiting my turn, as every superstar gets taken right before I pick. It's refreshing to know I can do something about each player, as long as I have enough money to keep bidding.

With an auction, however, you need to know how much money you have left, and what kind of financial shape the other owners are in. You also need to put on your poker face. You can't be so obvious bidding on a player that everyone knows you'll pay anything to get him. They'll use that knowledge to drive up the price.

There is a lot more strategy doing an auction compared to picking your players through a draft. In drafting, especially in the first round, it almost seems like the top players are slotted each season. Everybody has a good idea who the top ten picks are going to be. But in an auction league, prices can fluctuate. Comparable star players can go at wildly different dollar figures.

Dealing with Your Budget

Auction leagues are more skillful than draft leagues because you not only need to do your homework on players, but also maintain your economic budget. You may know the players better than your fellow owners, but if you're out of money there is nothing to do but sit and mope. You can't carry over leftover money. This isn't to say you shouldn't spend. The worst sin committed in auctions is to leave the table with unspent dollars. What were you waiting for? Too many times owners are left spending wildly at the end when there's not much left because they didn't spend enough before. Players like Vinny Testaverde, Michael Bennett, Michael Pittman, and Eddie George were going for astronomical sums at the end of my 2004 auction league because desperate owners had too much unused money.

A lot is determined by when a player's name comes up. His price can be inflated if brought up at the beginning of the auction, or at the end if a lot of owners have been hording their funds. On the other hand, bargains can often be found in the very beginning when owners may be hesitant to spend right away. Sometimes good prices can be discovered in the middle of the draft, when some owners have already spent too much while others are still laying back. Because you never know what might happen, you need to be vigilant at all times.

There are many different philosophies. Some will tell you that you should never spend more than 25 percent of your budget on a single player. Others say never go higher than 30 percent, while others move that figure to

40 percent on one player. Your bid obviously depends on how your league is structured. There are only a handful of impact players, so you'd like to get at least one of them. But you can't wildly overspend. In my auction league, for example, we have $280 in which to purchase twenty-five players. We start two quarterbacks, three running backs, three wide receivers, one tight end, two kickers, seven defensive players, and a utility player, who can be from any position. The six remaining players compose our **bench** or **taxi squad**, which is the rest of our players not in the starting lineup.

Strategies for Franchise Players

My approach is to spend big bucks on two running backs, while paying medium price for two other running backs. I'll invest the rest of my money on quarterbacks and wide receivers, while going cheap on kickers, a tight end, and defensive players. If you overspend in one area, though, you have to be financially prudent at other positions. I'm willing to go as high as $65 on a franchise running back. I've never had a problem getting one at that price. But be ready to spend early.

People bring up all the best players early because they want to drain money. It doesn't always work that way, because many owners are conservative during the beginning of the auction. I'd rather spend $35 on Tiki Barber and $21 on Warrick Dunn during the first forty-five minutes than get involved in a $38 bidding war for Steven Jackson during the fifth hour of the auction.

Yes, auctions are longer than drafts, especially when the roster size is twenty-five. You're not going to have enough money, or ammunition, to get the best running backs, quarterbacks, and wide receivers. I'd rather spend $50 getting Jake Plummer and Tom Brady than spend $65 for Peyton Manning and A.J. Feeley. I'd also rather invest $68 for three wide receivers—getting Joe Horn, Eric Moulds, and Chad Johnson all in the low $20s—than spend $45 apiece for Randy Moss, Marvin Harrison, and Terrell Owens. These are some of the strategies you can develop from following the past bidding habits of your fellow owners.

One effective strategy is to bring up good but non-franchise players early. For example, the first name I brought up in my 2004 draft was one of the decent kickers. No one wanted to spend money on a kicker in the beginning, so I got him for a cheap price. Later people started spending wildly on kickers, not wanting to get caught short on the position.

Injuries are so common in football that it is too much of a gamble to invest heavily in just one or two players. It's always great to get value. Realistically, however, it's not going to happen if your league has more than ten owners. You might be able to get a good price on a player, but you're not going to come away from an auction stealing any player. If you wait too long, hoping for a super bargain, you're going to get left out. Yes, some owners will run out of money early enough that they won't be a factor during the middle to latter portion of the auction, but there will still be enough owners left with

DRAFT AND AUCTION STRATEGIES

money to make a difference and keep prices in line. Don't expect otherwise.

Prepare for the Auction

It's vital to monitor how the auction proceeds. The barometer is often set at the beginning. Before the auction, decide on each player's price. Be realistic about the figure. Player values can fluctuate depending on the scoring system your league uses, roster size, and the personalities of your league owners. Make sure the dollar amounts you assigned to each player add up to the total amount of money that all teams spend.

Then see if the auction is following that pattern. If stars are going for less, then there's going to be a correction later. So now is the time to buy. If owners are overpaying early, keep a low profile. Make your move in the middle or end of the auction when there are better buys. Just make sure all the top players aren't gone by then. Remember not to panic. Figuring there are about twenty to twenty-five blue-chippers each year, you have ample opportunity to get your share. You don't have to bite at the first big name called out—unless, of course, there's a bargain to be had.

Playing the Dollar End Game

In auction formats you need to have a deep list at each position. Because I spend so much on the skill positions, I find myself heavily involved in what I call the $1 end game. This is where your maximum bid can only be $1 because you've spent the rest of your funds. You can't bid more than a $1 if you have $5 remaining and need to acquire five players. Purchase three good running backs, a solid quarterback and a couple of "B" wide receivers and you're not going to have a whole lot left of your bankroll.

The strategy of some owners is not to pay big on any one player, but instead come away with a roster full of solid starters. That's fine, but if you can get your share of superstars, plus solid players for $1, that's even better. To accomplish this, though, you need to study, study, and study more. I can get away with this approach in my league because we start seven defensive players. I pride myself on knowing defensive players as well as I know the skill position players. This is tough for some owners because aside from statistics on tackles and sacks leaders, information isn't as readily available on defensive players.

Defensive coordinators come and go. So do new systems. This makes for a lot of sleepers on defense because roles change. Owners are going to be reluctant to spend more than $1 on somebody they're not familiar with, or a player they're not sure of. You have to be more careful if you're in a league where each player's statistics count and there are no bench players. In this situation, you don't want to be in a position of having to pick up $1 players—it's just too risky.

Bidding Strategies

You should focus on two main goals at an auction: getting the players you want, and making the other owners pay top dollar for the rest of the players. Obviously everyone wants the superstars. There are no secrets there. After that, things get more subjective. It helps to mix up your play. This means sometimes bringing up a player you really want.

Some owners actually do this a lot. One owner admitted that anybody he nominates early is somebody he desperately wants. Guys can admit many things to each other in the interest of bonding and friendship, but never reveal anything to anybody when it comes to fantasy football. Some things, like bidding tactics, are better left alone.

Because of the bidding process, more strategy comes into play in auction leagues. Different tactics can all be effective. For example, there are some players I absolutely don't want. I'll often throw their names out when it is my turn to nominate a player. But be careful doing this. Don't open with a bid that no one else will top, but also don't open with a ridiculously low bid.

Some owners always start a player's name out with a bid of $1, even if he is a superstar. This only slows down the auction. Saying, "Peyton Manning for one dollar," might be funny the first time, but it's not humorous after that. You want people to pay big on players you have no interest in. To achieve that purpose you need to have proper timing. That's why superstars are often thrown out first.

You have to gauge not only the prices that have been going on the players, but the positions as well. For instance, I had no interest in Eddie George during our 2004 auction. I knew a couple of owners in the league favored veteran runners, and saw that a few owners needed running backs and there weren't that many left.

So fairly late in the auction, I brought up George's name with a $5 bid. This was showing everyone that I didn't consider George to be a $1 player. Actually, I really did. But I knew at that juncture of the auction there would be fierce bidding on a running back that was perceived as a starter at the time. So I wasn't in any danger of actually getting stuck with George. Quickly the bidding escalated. George ended up going for $27. There's no way he would have gone for that ridiculous sum if his name had been called earlier.

Bidding can get competitive. But don't ever get caught up in an ego war, believing you have to get this player or that player. Always have a backup plan or contingency if the price goes too high on a player you really wanted. If an owner badly wants a player, sometimes it will show in his face. He'll have an exasperated or grim expression as the bidding goes up and up, or his voice will rise and his tone will turn more strident. These are all tells. So is the cadence in an owner's voice. If it changes, he could be ready to quit bidding, or is just trying to string other bidders along.

Look for physical giveaways. For example, a clenched fist could mean renewed determination. One owner in my league starts rocking in his chair whenever he really wants a player. He's not even aware of it. Another owner rises in his chair. It's not to the point where you want to wear sunglasses indoors, like some do in the World Series of Poker, but you should still try not to give anything away. I'll mix up my bids, change my voice inflections on purpose, and smile a lot just to keep owners from trying to read me.

There can be a lot of disinformation out there. Don't always believe an owner if he tells you how high he is on a player. A lot of deception goes around before a fantasy draft or auction. Some owners stay loyal to the players on their favorite team. If that's the case, make them pay extra to land their desired star players. If you know one owner who loves the Packers, don't drop out of the bidding so fast for Ahman Green and Brett Favre. Those aren't bad players to have. On the other hand, let a Packer fan have Bubba Franks or the team's number three wideout if he wants them so badly.

Keep Track of Opponent's Budgets

Being involved in an auction process is kind of like being a military commander. You need to know your enemy's position. That means keeping track of everyone's finances—not just your own. At some point toward the end of an auction, owners can only bid up to a certain amount on a player because they need to fill out their rosters. They wouldn't have enough cash left if they bid too high. Be aware of that and exploit it. Try to use your reserves—money you have been holding back—to get players before there's a drop in talent levels. For me, that means getting that last "B" wide receiver if the price is in the ballpark, or spending an extra dollar to get a mid-level quarterback when the rest are borderline starters or backups.

Stay Flexible

Some owners set up specific budgets per position. You can have a financial game plan, but things rarely go accordingly and you need to be adaptable. If good kickers and defenses happen to be undervalued areas, be flexible enough to take one. Just make sure you don't get caught short at the skill positions. Part of your game plan should be keeping a list of potential break-out players who might be undervalued. Don't overpay for these guys, but if a bunch of them haven't been called out yet, keep enough funds in reserve to get at least a couple of them. I don't like to bring these guys up until near the end, when there's not a lot of money left, and only then if most of the owners don't need any more players at that particular position.

Post-Auction Deals

Attitudes can be a lot different after an auction compared to a draft. After a draft, some owners get a little cocky, believing they have the best team. Not so with an auction. Sure, everybody should come away with several superstars, but no one roped in all the players they bid on. If you're overloaded at a position, but could use help in another area, check the rosters and see if any owners have some excess at that spot. Chances are they do.

It happens, too, that you can come away with a player at the end of the auction who the rest of the league forgot about. Don't be afraid to talk up that player, like I did following my 2004 auction when I said, "I can't believe I got Marcus Robinson for a dollar at the end. He's going to have a monster year with Randy Moss being double and triple teamed all the time." Perhaps an owner will bite and offer you a favorable deal right then. No need to mention Robinson's history of being fragile and inconsistent.

Keep Learning

After the auction, when everybody is happily exhausted and relaxed, it is a good time to pick owners' brains about how they rated their players. They'll have their guard down and will feel like talking. This can possibly give you some insight into what players might go for the following year. Be shrewd about it, though. Consider beginning the conversation by saying, "Boy, you got a nice price on so-and-so." Appreciating the compliment and your interest in his roster, the owner might open up to you, revealing his thinking. Keep his statements stored in your memory if he does. It might come in very handy the following year when you're bidding against him.

DRAFT VS. AUCTION FORMAT

Which is better? Both draft and auction styles have their pluses and minuses. It really depends upon the participants and their experience level. Most leagues use draft.

The major disadvantage of a draft format is that you're not assured of getting a player you really want. In fact, if you have a low first round pick, it's very likely all the top running backs and quarterbacks will be gone by the time your pick finally comes around. You should be able to get two solid players with your first two choices, but chances are, any dominant players have already been picked. It's a real drawback if you're choosing last in leagues with more than twelve owners.

That was the number one complaint I heard about high-end money leagues where some owners, who had to ante up more than $1,000 for the entry fee, ended up picking last in competition with thirteen other owners. They thought that was too much of a disadvantage, arguing that no high-end league should have more than twelve owners. There are a limited number of franchise players. Once you get into the second round, the draft becomes more subjective when there is a much wider range of opinions.

One guy in our Rotisserie draft league landed the number one pick two straight years. He took Priest Holmes each time and consequently finished first in touchdowns each year. Luckily he wasn't one of the more skillful owners and he didn't place in the money. Still, it was frustrating to see the same guy keep lucking out and getting Holmes.

With an auction format you can get any player you want, if you're willing to spend the bucks. The best running backs are there for every owner to fight for. In an auction, each owner gets a bankroll to acquire his team. You can strategize, targeting certain players or positions. You can't do that in drafts since they are so random. Another advantage to auction leagues is that you don't have to worry about position runs, like you do in a draft. You can step in and purchase without having to sit frustrated, waiting, seemingly forever, for your turn.

Auction leagues, though, are more complex. You're now dealing with economics and keeping track of money. So you not only need to do your homework on players, but math becomes a factor, too. Sharp auction owners keep track not only of their money, but also everyone else's. You don't want to leave money on the table. On the other hand, you don't want to be in a spot where you're down to spending just $1 on each player and still have ten positions to fill.

If you're doing an auction league, you need to find an auctioneer. The auctioneer should have a strong voice and consistence cadence. You can usually recruit a friend by having everyone in the league chip in to buy him a meal before or during the auction. Notice the word meal and not beer. Sober people make the best auctioneers.

Our auction league is handled by an owner who competes in a draft league. He enjoys being the auctioneer because it gives him a better feel on where players could be drafted, and how highly regarded certain sleepers are. It's a good argument to use if you need to recruit an owner in another league to be your auctioneer.

KEEPER LEAGUE STRATEGY

Keeper leagues are where you retain some of your players from one year to the next. These players are called **keepers**. Non-keeper leagues begin new each season. With a keeper league you're active the entire year because you already have some of your players to watch and monitor.

Once you know which players you're holding on to, you should attempt to deal any decent players left on your roster before your draft or auction. The operative word here is decent. Don't waste someone's time offering a borderline keeper for a superstar. Bad trade offers hurt your credibility. If you're unsure of a player's value, float out his name as a trial balloon. Posting a message on your league bulletin board and sending out a league-wide e-mail are easy ways to communicate. If you happen to have four quality running backs or two upper tier quarterbacks and can only keep one at each position, check everyone's roster to see who desperately needs another running back or quarterback. Then make an individual pitch. It's worth your while to gain an extra draft pick or top wide receiver in return.

Teams that fall out of contention are often primed to make a deal during the season. They might be willing to trade their best player for two excellent keeper prospects. A deal like this can be beneficial to both owners. The contending owner gets stronger, while the owner who is playing for the following season gets a prime keeper or two. If you're going to concede your season and start thinking keepers, make sure you don't do it prematurely. One keeper league owner opened the year with a 2-5 record. Thinking he had no shot, he dealt a couple of his best players for rookies. But he had a better team than he thought. He won seven of his next eight matches to finish 9-6, barely missing his league's playoffs.

You have the bargaining advantage if you're the team playing for next season. You can afford to be patient. The team dangling potential keepers trying to win the current season has far more urgency. So don't necessarily accept the first trade offer, unless it's too good to refuse. Let all the contenders know that you're considering playing for next season and would be willing to deal a stud for draft picks or a certain player or two. Then see what kind of offers come in.

There's no need to be in a rush. One nice thing about being around the bottom of the standings is that you get an early crack at the free agent pool. Often you can find bargains there, and players who have a chance to make an impact the following season.

I always try to keep a few keeper candidates on my roster. That way I have ammunition either way. When trying to win a league title in keeper leagues, you need to aggressively target those owners who have no shot at winning but might have one or two good players that could push you over the top. Be tactful, though, when approaching these owners. Nobody likes to be told they can't win. Let them pick out who they like on your team. If it's somebody you can afford to trade, then make the deal. But in this situation, you're not looking for a fair deal. You're willing to give them something that may help their team the following year, but you have to get a sure thing in return.

If you're the team playing for the following season, target which players would be the best keepers the following year. Don't get caught up on how well they're playing this season. Try to project their talent, potential, and production for the following year. Case in point was

Willis McGahee in 2004. He was taken late, or for a low amount in many auction leagues, because he didn't open the season as the Bills starting running back.

But if you discount the first third of the season when he played sparingly behind Travis Henry, McGahee would have finished with the fourth-highest scoring average among running backs based on his excellent second half production. So McGahee makes a prime keeper candidate, especially since his injured knee still wasn't quite 100 percent in 2004. He figures to get even better. That's scary. If a team fighting for first had McGahee in a keeper league, they were in a great spot to deal.

The toughest decision you'll make in keeper leagues are who to protect and who to throw back into the pool. You need to evaluate different variables. Ask yourself these questions: Is this player still in his prime? Do his prospects look better or worse for a bigger season next season? How much of an upside does he have? Is he injury prone? You also need to take into account position scarcity. What happens, for instance, if you don't protect a running back? How many good ones will be available? It's the same with quarterbacks. If you have to make a decision between two players you're torn on, see which one has better trade value.

Your league format definitely comes into play when making these decisions. Understand your league scoring system. Some players are more valuable in yardage-type leagues; others are worth more in leagues weighted more toward touchdowns. Kerry Collins always throws for a lot of yards, but those yards don't translate into touchdowns.

Edgerrin James finished fourth in rushing in 2004, but scored fewer touchdowns than ten other backs. Laveranues Coles caught 90 passes in 2004, seventh highest in the NFL. But Coles only scored one touchdown. Brandon Stokley, on the other hand, hauled in 22 fewer passes than Coles, but scored nine more touchdowns.

In keeper leagues, where an auction is used to acquire players, price becomes a major consideration in protection. That's the way my keeper league works. So I'm always on the lookout for undervalued players, or anyone whose salary is lower than what the perceived norm should be. Some owners have a different philosophy. They'll keep a superstar no matter what his salary. Most of these big names, though, are overpriced. I'd rather protect low-salaried players with high ceiling and have more bucks to spend at the auction than a player at or above value. With that in mind, I traded a $21 Eric Moulds late in the 2004 season for a $4 Roy Williams.

I'm always looking to deal any overpriced star in order to get value in return. That's part of the fun of being in a keeper league. You can talk trade all year round.

RECOGNIZING RUNS

The term **runs** is frequently used when owners start gobbling up players at a certain position during the draft. It can happen at any point, at any position. It's not uncommon to see many running backs picked in a row. In my 2003 league, for instance, the first fourteen picks all were running backs before someone broke the logjam taking Randy Moss with his second-round pick.

Instead of a normal flow where players from each position get chosen, runs can occur when owners start panicking. In the middle rounds, for instance, they might get scared that there could become a shortage of quality quarterbacks or wide receivers. Because of that, eight wide receivers might be drafted in a row. It's not uncommon to see late runs on kickers and defenses. Owners don't want to get caught short at any position.

It's also fairly common to see a run on wide receivers in round three if most owners used their first two picks on running backs. It's the same with "B" level quarterbacks in rounds four and five. So what should you do? Be a sheep and just follow the herd, or continue to look for value, and if the value isn't at that position, go another direction?

Your draft position is important. It matters what spot you're drafting from. If you're picking in the middle you're protected. You shouldn't get caught short if a run happens because there aren't that many players picked before you get to draft again. The end spots—picking in the first or last spot—are more dangerous because you could get left out. You're vulnerable if a run starts right after you pick because in twelve-owner leagues, you can wait twenty-two picks until your turn again. It's similar with drafting at number two or in the second-to-last spot. But even in these positions, I rarely like to start a run on a position. Let someone else do it.

I'm not worried if runs get started on wide receiver, defense, and tight end because there are enough to go around. Instead of reaching too early for a defense, tight end, or just grabbing the next "C" wide receiver, I would check if any quality running backs are still available. However, if you need to protect yourself because there is only a small group of good players left before there's a huge drop off at a position, then follow the run if it's at that particular position. Many times, though, if I can't get the best or second-best player at a position, I'm content to wait because there rarely is a consensus on the best wide receiver, tight end, defense, and kicker after the top two or three are drafted.

Sometimes you can defend against runs by anticipating when they're going to occur. If the first two rounds are top-heavy with running backs and quarterbacks, then figure a lot of wide receivers are going to fall in round three. If mostly running backs and wide receivers were picked during the first three rounds, then probably a lot of quarterbacks are going to get called out in round four. If you're picking late in round four and you're worried there won't be a strong enough quarterback for you, then choose one in the third round. You never want to get caught short at quarterback. Consequently, if there are still eight quarterbacks you like and several teams picking in front of you already have their quarterbacks, then it's probably safe to wait another round before grabbing one.

There are always kicker runs in my face-to-face league. During the 2004 season the run on kickers started in the ninth round. Since we go twenty-five rounds, I thought this was too early. But kicking is a category and we have to play two kickers. Some like to have a third kicker to cover bye weeks and have as an option at the utility or flex position. In round nine there were eight straight kickers picked. Then in round ten, six more kickers were selected. Still available were Emmitt Smith, Eddie George, Jimmy Smith, and Rod Smith, along with decent number three wide receivers, good tight ends, and quarterbacks Drew Brees and Kerry Collins.

It helps to know your fellow owners in anticipating runs. One owner, for instance, almost always takes the first kicker in one of my leagues. If he's picking at the top or end, he'll take the first two kickers. He did it a couple of years in the fifth and six rounds. That was way too early. The next kicker didn't go until four rounds later. So no run occurred there. If an owner makes a mistake by taking a kicker or defense too soon, then the chances are good that you don't have to worry about a run taking place at that juncture.

This owner was picking in the middle of the pack this past season and took Jason Elam in the ninth round. The next owner followed suit by taking a kicker. That started the stampede. The next six selections were all kickers. If you were picking at the top and wanted an elite kicker, you needed to estimate at what point the owner might make his kicking move. So it's worth saving your draft sheets if you play with the same owners each year. Study their likes and dislikes. Know the time frame they target certain positions. That way you can launch a preemptive strike and avoid getting caught short when there's a position scarcity.

HANDCUFF STRATEGY

I'm not a big fan of **handcuffing**, which is taking the backup to a star player you drafted earlier. I'm more open-minded to it if I'm only investing a late-round draft pick. I always mutter a sarcastic, "yeah right" whenever I read or hear someone talking about handcuffing a backup to his starter. Just about every preseason fantasy article on Marshall Faulk in 2004 ended with the following "… and don't forget to handcuff Steven Jackson to Faulk."

The problem is that it's not so easy to get Jackson or any other prominent backup running back. You're usually competing against nine to thirteen other owners to get that player. Chances are they all know about Jackson and other promising backups.

If I had drafted an aging Faulk in 2004, I would have loved to take Jackson for insurance, but only if I hadn't had to reach higher than I normally would to get him. I had Jackson rated as a "C" tier running back during his rookie season. Once all the "B" runners were gone, I would consider Jackson. But if I had drafted Faulk I wouldn't have jumped Jackson ahead of any runners I rated higher. In the case of Priest Holmes, LaDainian Tomlinson, and Deuce McAllister in 2004, you probably could have gotten their backups in the final round. That's because at the time, few—if any—owners were interested in their backups: Derrick Blaylock, Jessie Chatman, and Aaron Stecker. All three ended up seeing more playing time than expected. A lot, too, depends on the quality of the backup.

Handcuffing is one of those fantasy football catchphrases. I find it very overrated. It's just as easy to get burned from it as it is to win with it. In one of my 2004 leagues I drafted Lee Suggs in the third round. Then three rounds later I took the Browns' other running back, William Green, as the handcuff. In the beginning it was working out. Suggs was hurt at the start of the season, so Green got the bulk of the carries. But the first time they were both healthy, it was difficult to decide which one to start. I went with Green because then-Browns Coach Butch Davis said Green would remain the starter.

Sure enough, Green started, but then Davis proceeded to use Suggs nearly the entire game at the expense of Green. I lost my head-to-head match that week by one point. Davis said he just forgot to put Green back in the game. His plan had been to play them both equally. He later apologized to Green for not putting him back in the second half. I'm still waiting for Davis to apologize to me. I shed no tears when Butch was ushered out in Cleveland. Good riddance.

As things turned out during much of the season, Davis split the carries between Green and Suggs, destroying their fantasy impact. You cannot have your third-round draft pick being a part-time starter and expect to win a league. It was a similar story in Buffalo during 2004 when Travis Henry had the bulk of the carries in the first half of the season, then gave way to Willis McGahee. I had even worse luck trying to decipher the Broncos running back situation in 2004. In my draft and auction league I went for Quentin Griffin and handcuffed Tatum Bell to him in both leagues.

So what happened?

Griffin lost his starting spot and then got hurt and was out for the year. Bell wasn't yet ready to be full-time, so Broncos Coach Mike Shanahan turned to unheralded fullback Reuben Droughns, making him the featured back. So my fifth and eight round draft picks were rendered meaningless, while some lucky bungler at the bottom of the standings got to pluck the Broncos' new main runner off the free agent wire.

This is another danger to handcuffing. You can pick the wrong backup. In the case of the Vikings, it turned out that fourth-string rookie Mewelde Moore would make just as big an impact as any of their other running backs during the 2004 season. It was Moore who finished with more rushing yards than injury-prone Michael Bennett and one-dimensional Moe Williams, averaging an impressive 5.8 yards a carry.

So if you're not 100 percent sure who the main backup is, don't handcuff. I wouldn't handcuff unless you believe that the backup is a good player in his own right, and then only take him in what you consider the proper round. Don't jump the gun and reach. If he goes, he goes. Too many times you're stuck with a backup who never gets to play. This happens far too often. Believe me. I remember sitting on Saints reserve running back Curtis Keaton nearly the entire 2002 season because I thought starter Deuce McAllister would get hurt since he often had been banged up when he played college ball. McAllister ended up carrying 325 times that season. Keaton had all of 12 carries. By clinging to the worthless Keaton, I wasted a draft pick, used up a valuable bench spot, and reduced my options of who to start at the flex position. I would have been better served taking Buster Keaton instead of Curtis Keaton. At least that way I might have gotten a laugh instead of being laughed at.

You're better off taking a starting wide receiver, an "A" kicker, or upper tier defense before reaching for the backup of a stud running back. Insurance is nice in fantasy football but the price has to be right.

DRAFTING TRADE BAIT

It seems to happen every year. This past season it was Anquan Boldin. In 2003 it was Michael Vick and Chad Pennington. A key player gets hurt in the preseason or during practice and is out the first couple of months of the season.

When should you look to draft that player, if at all? Michael Vick missing four games, one-fourth of the season, isn't nearly as good as having Michael Vick for the entire season. You never know if the player will be fully healthy when returning. People seem to assume they will, especially when they've been waiting so long for that player. But it's not a given. It didn't happen with Vikings running back Michael Bennett until late in the 2004 season after Bennett was injured right before the season. Those who took Bennett got burned.

Unless it's a keeper league, or a league that allows trading, I would stay away from injured players at the draft. With so many good players available during the first few rounds, there's no reason to take a chance when you don't have to. If the injured player is a top running back or quarterback and still hasn't been picked by the middle rounds, then I would take him, provided he's not going to be out more than two months. But we have to be talking about a superstar here. I'm not using a middle round draft pick on an injured Charlie Garner or suspended Michael Pittman.

It doesn't make any sense to draft an injured player if you're not getting value. Vick, for instance, would have been a first or second round draft pick in 2003. But he suffered a broken leg during preseason. So his draft status and auction value plummeted. While normal superstar quarterbacks in our keeper auction league were going for $35 to $50, Vick went for $26. Not enough value for me. But I was bidding on him at $18, and would have taken him around the eighth round in our draft league if he hadn't gone in the sixth round.

The thinking on taking an injured superstar isn't to have a great second-stringer down the road. You should already have a serviceable starter at your skill position spots. But taking a recuperating superstar later than when he normally would have been picked gives you an under-valued player in keeper leagues, and a player who makes excellent trade bait in non-keeper leagues.

Trading an injured player can be tricky, though. First, no owner is going to offer much until the player returns. Would you take damaged goods in a trade? Once the player returns you may need to be patient. It only takes one owner to consumate a trade, but the rest of the league knows you're looking to move that player because you're probably overloaded at that position. Essentially you could be the one held hostage.

So, what to do? First target those owners lowest in the standings. They could be desperate, or in a panic mode, willing to do anything to shake up their team. The problem with them is that they usually have injuries, too, or don't have that many good players. Also look to deal your now-healthy star player to an owner who needs help at that position.

Be aware that good, "B" wide receivers such as Boldin probably aren't going to fetch much in return. There are far more solid wide receivers than running backs and quarterbacks. Wide receivers also don't get hurt as frequently as quarterbacks and running backs, so other owners aren't as desperate for them.

If you're coming up on the trade deadline and still haven't had any luck dealing your returning injured player you can do two things. The first is to just sit on the player. That's what one owner did who drafted Michael Vick in his 2003 keeper league. His starting quarterback was Steve McNair, who was the NFL's Co-Most Valuable Player that year with Peyton Manning. The owner traded Vick during the off-season after finally finding an offer he liked.

The second option is to bite the bullet and basically give the player away for the best offer. That's tough to do. But if you're chasing a league title and can get some help at a position that needs strengthening, even if it's just a little, make the trade. Accept that it wasn't what you were hoping to get, but at least it upgrades your team. Some owners can't do that. They insist on getting equal or better value for what they're offering.

You have to be flexible and consider the circumstances and reality of the situation. A healthy Michael Vick may be worth an "A" running back, but if you can't make that deal and need more depth at running back with the trade deadline clock ticking down, don't be stubborn enough to pass on getting some help. If you're going to stress about what to do with your injured player, then don't take him in the first place.

Your last choice is to just hold on to the player. At least then you have flexibility and insurance at the position, and depending on your league rules, you might be able to use him in your flex spot.

SLEEPERS AND BUSTS

These two expressions have become so common they almost are clichés. Yet, what exactly is the definition of a sleeper and a bust?

Sleepers

I define a **sleeper** as a player with a lot of promise and potential who most people aren't entirely familiar with yet. If a player is rated among the top 50 he's not a sleeper. Some considered Willis McGahee a sleeper because he sat out the 2003 season. But McGahee was no sleeper going into 2004. He was the Bills' number one pick in 2003, a high-profile running back from the University of Miami. He already had caught the imagination of many fantasy football owners before his first NFL carry.

Real sleepers are low-profile players expected to do little going into a season, but given an opportunity emerge as viable fantasy performers. Examples of such players from 2004 include T.J. Houshmandzadeh, Reuben Droughns, Nate Burleson, and Ronald Curry. None of these players was drafted in many fantasy leagues. Most sleepers aren't taken in the draft unless there are more than eighteen rounds. They come from the free agent pool.

It's hard to find legitimate sleepers like this nowadays with so much information available. That's why the term sleeper might even be obsolete. A genuine sleeper isn't someone who had a surprisingly big year, like Muhsin Muhammad, Javon Walker, Jake Delhomme, and Drew Bennett did in 2004. While these players probably were all undervalued in most leagues, and taken late in drafts, they were known commodities. They just performed above expectations.

Everybody had these guys on their draft lists, although some ranked very low. A true sleeper is somebody totally unexpected having a fine year. It's easy to find sleepers on defense in leagues drafting seven to ten defensive players, using tackles and sacks as categories. There weren't too many fantasy owners who were on Lance Briggs, Antonio Pierce, Cato June, Danny Clark, D.J. Williams, Kevin Williams, James Hall, and Reggie Hayward before the 2004 draft.

You can find semi-sleepers at wide receiver and tight end. It is doubtful that rookie Michael Clayton and Antonio Gates were taken in every 2004 draft. Both Clayton and Gates had early opportunities to make an imprint. Clayton took advantage of numerous Buccaneer wide receiver injuries and Keenan McCardell's holdout to catch 80 passes for 1,193 yards, while Gates was on a Chargers squad that didn't have any stud wide receivers.

It's almost impossible to find a sleeper at quarterback and running back. Any rookie taken in the first three rounds of the NFL draft is immediately scrutinized and heavily dissected. It's a great feeling to hit on a sleeper. Be warned, though—many sleeper picks don't work out. For every Houshmandzadeh and Droughns there are many more Bethel Johnsons, Tyrone Calicos, Tony Hollings, Doug Gabriels, ReShard Lees, and Brock Forseys. You tend to remember the successes and forget about the embarrassing failures.

Busts

The definition for **bust** is less subjective. It's a player who doesn't live up to his press clippings, expectations, and potential. Ryan Leaf, of course, is the all-time bust quarterback. Actually Leaf would have been a great pickup if interceptions, temper tantrums, and upsetting teammates were fantasy categories. Kerry Collins would be the number one quarterback if turnovers counted instead of touchdowns.

Usually you can't get too hurt gambling on a sleeper. Because chances are, you've only invested a late-round draft choice or picked him from the free agent pool as a temporary replacement. Not so with a bust. They can really ruin your team. For the first time ever I didn't finish in the money in my face-to-face draft league during the 2004 season. A big reason why is because I made Kevan Barlow my second round draft choice, the number thirteen overall selection. There were twenty-five players who rushed for more yards than Barlow in 2004.

Fortunately most busts don't fail as miserably as Leaf, or decide to unexpectedly retire right before the season as Ricky Williams did. There are high-profile busts like Lawrence Phillips, Blair Thomas, and Heath Shuler. More common are busts that had a little success before flaming out. These are players who were drafted high, possessed intriguing talent, and may even have briefly put up decent numbers, but never fulfilled their lofty expectations.

There are many reasons why a player can become a bust. Injuries, for one. Donte Stallworth always seems to have a pulled hamstring or groin. Michael Bennett and Panthers linebacker Dan Morgan constantly get injured. It gets to the point where you no longer want these guys on your roster, no matter how high their skill level. A popular refrain heard going into the 2005 season is, "I will never take Michael Bennett again."

Sometimes the player is in the wrong system or is a head case. Steve McNair's passing statistics were limited his first four years as a starter because the Titans were a run-oriented team. Jeff Garcia, a top fantasy-producing quarterback with the 49ers, struggled in his only season with the Browns because the team lacked an offensive identity.

When it comes to busts, though, sometimes you have to take responsibility and admit that you blew it. You were expecting too much and drafted the player too high. Fantasy owners were excited when Peerless Price was traded from the Bills to the Falcons. They targeted him high in their draft, figuring he would have a breakout season now that he would be the top receiving option after being number two behind Eric Moulds for four years from 1999 to 2002. But going into 2005, Price has yet to show he's worthy of being a number one wide receiver.

Don't be too hard on yourself if some of your late-round picks turn out to be busts. Often you're just taking a flyer on a late-round pick. If it hits, great; if not, you'll soon pick up a replacement player for him in the free agent pool. Aim high. There's little to lose. Just don't have unreasonable expectations if it doesn't work. Just because some team might be foolish enough to anoint Tyrone Wheatley their starting tailback, doesn't suddenly mean he's going to stay healthy and rush for 1,500 yards.

THIRTEEN ESSENTIAL RULES TO REMEMBER

Fantasy football is full of things to do and don't. Here's a lucky list of thirteen.

1. Don't overanalyze the preseason. It's basically worthless. You're just sweating it out, hoping that your players don't get hurt. Anybody foolish enough to take preseason statistics seriously should learn a lesson from 2002 when the Redskins went 4-1 in exhibition play under Steve Spurrier, sparked by the immortal duo of

quarterback Danny Wuerffel and wide receiver Derrius Thompson. You don't want to overrate backups battling for roster spots, or underrate proven veterans whose stats aren't very good during preseason.

2. Do know your league's scoring system. It makes a difference if passing touchdowns count four or six points, if receptions count as one point or half a point, if bonus points are awarded for length of touchdowns or going above certain yardage figures, and if you can lose points for turnovers.

3. Don't get intimidated. Fantasy football is a simple game. Some people can talk a big game, but injuries and your own feel on players are the determining factors. John Culligan and David Eads won the 2004 World Championship of Fantasy Football and the $200,000 that went with it by not being intimidated. The pair helped work on the 2003 WCOFF draft thinking they would be so impressed by the skill level of the 652 participants in the high-end contest and perhaps learn some things. They soon realized the competitors weren't that good. "After watching what went on, I told John, 'You know, I don't think these guys are all that sharp,'" Eads told fantasy sports columnist Kevin Iole in a *Las Vegas Review-Journal* story.

4. Do trust your gut. Prepare for the draft by reading and listening, using everything at your disposal. But in the end make your own decisions. It's your team, after all. Whether you end up right or wrong, at least you played your own opinions. Keep an open mind. If you don't think running back is the way to go, then take a quarterback or receiver. Few people could have envisioned quarterbacks finishing as the top three point-scorers in many fantasy leagues during 2004.

5. Don't get caught short at running backs. The supply of starting running backs is much shorter than at the other positions. If you decide not to take one during the first two rounds, you better start loading up fast. This isn't a game of chicken. You need to seriously address your running back situation before it gets out of hand. Going into a fantasy matchup with Ladell Betts and Travis Minor as your starting runners is not exactly a proven formula for success.

6. Do stay on top of injuries. This applies to both before the draft and during the season. It took Edgerrin James more than two seasons to fully come back from a knee injury. Just because a player returns from an injury doesn't automatically mean he can pick up right where he left off. Stay vigilant. This means double-checking the latest news and staying aware of all injuries right until you have to submit your lineup. Late scratches really hurt those owners with early starting lineup deadlines who had Stephen Davis, Duce Staley, and Chris Brown in 2004.

7. Don't ever say no to taking a particular player, no matter how mad you may be at that player. Tiki Barber is proof of that. After Barber scored just two touchdowns and fumbled five times in 2003, one owner crossed Barber off his 2004 list, even though he could have gotten him at a good spot in the draft. Barber came back to set career highs in rushing with 1,518 yards and touchdowns with 13. He also only lost two fumbles. There is an exception to this suggestion: His name is Michael Bennett.

8. Don't take a defense too high. It's too hit or miss. You're talking about eleven guys. If a certain area or key player goes down with injuries, it can collapse everything. Even if the defense plays well there's no guarantee of picking up big points because the offense can give up points via a turnover or special teams can allow a score.

9. Don't get discouraged if your early picks fail to put up big numbers. Culligan and Eads captured their WCOFF title despite taking Jamal Lewis in the first round and having disap-

pointing Matt Hasselbeck as their quarterback. Lewis missed four games, while only scoring more than one touchdown in a game one time. For the 2004 season he scored just seven times, barely finishing above 1,000 yards rushing. Lewis had double the touchdowns and more than double the rushing yards during his record-breaking 2003 season. Hasselbeck finished fourteenth in passing yards and nine quarterbacks threw for more touchdowns.

10. Do expect the unexpected. Or as Emmitt Smith once put it, keep an eye open for the "diamond in the trash." In fantasy terms, the trash is the waiver wire and free agent pool. In 2004 you could have found Drew Brees, Billy Volek, Nick Goings, Reuben Droughns, Larry Johnson, and Nate Burleson residing there. You just never know.

11. Don't decide who to start based on which games are being nationally televised. Just because the Lions play on Thanksgiving doesn't mean Joey Harrington suddenly is a stud quarterback and worthy of playing that week. Yeah, it's fun to be able to watch your players perform, but it's more satisfying and rewarding to win your league.

12. Don't get impatient after one or two games. It's a four-month season. Give each player a

fair opportunity before yanking his butt or dealing him. Just remember, the week you trade him is the week he plays his best game. It happens a lot. On the other hand, don't keep sitting on a disappointing player when it has become obvious that for whatever reasons, he's not going to produce like you expected. After six consecutive years of gaining at least 1,100 yards, five-time Pro Bowl back Ricky Watters rushed for just 318 yards for the Seahawks in 2001. Watters had shoulder and ankle injuries that season. The Seahawks went with Shaun Alexander, in his second year then, and phased out Watters. Watters never gained another yard. A player's career can end just like that, even a former first-round fantasy running back like Watters.

13. Don't worry about your opponent's lineup. There's nothing you can do about it, short of bribing him to start Kordell Stewart instead of Donovan McNabb, which would look a tad suspicious. Just stick to playing your best starters. If your opponent happens to be starting Jaguars quarterback Byron Left-wich, don't insert some low-tier Jacksonville wide receiver like Troy Edwards to counter Leftwich's stats at the expense of much better wideouts on your team. Hopefully, of course, you've never had Troy Edwards on your roster. I made a bad decision last season

benching Brett Favre in favor of Brian Griese because my opponent that week was starting Packer wide receivers Javon Walker and Donald Driver. I let that determine my decision even though Favre was my starter, and two out of three times would have better stats than Griese, including that week.

7. THEORIES

There are many theories as to the best way to construct your fantasy football team. I will discuss a few of the major ones below.

SUPERSTAR THEORY

There are several **superstar** or **stud** theories. The main one is this: don't mess with your first-round pick. Draft a superstar and leave him in your lineup. Don't take him out—no matter what the matchup or how much he might be slumping—leave him in the game. The only exceptions, of course, are his bye week or if he is injured.

Case in point: Priest Holmes. He was the number one overall choice in 2004, as he should be after scoring 48 touchdowns the past two years. But in Week 7 of the 2004 season, Holmes's owners faced a choice. Priest hadn't topped 75 yards rushing his past two games, and that Sunday was going against the Falcons. The Falcons entered the matchup ranked number one in rush defense, allowing just 74 yards on the ground. No running back had gained 100 yards on them all season. What to do? Stick with your superstar, that's what.

Holmes rushed for 139 yards and scored four touchdowns against the Falcons in little more than a half before exiting in the third quarter with an ankle injury.

THEORIES

In a ten-owner league there are enough superstars to go around. The most reliable are the tough ones who rarely get injured such as Peyton Manning, LaDainian Tomlinson, Clinton Portis, Daunte Culpepper, and Shaun Alexander. Sometimes an owner is tempted to deviate from the norm when an intriguing talent is available even though that player has yet to reach proven star status. This can happen as early as the seventh pick. Most drafts in 2004 followed a similar pattern. The top six picks almost seemed slotted: Holmes, Tomlinson, Ahman Green, Portis, Alexander, and Deuce McAllister.

The choice at number seven came down to Edgerrin James, Jamal Lewis, or Randy Moss. James was the safest choice, being a stud running back and three years removed from his knee surgery. Lewis would have been a no-brainer at that spot, coming off a year where he rushed for the second most yards in NFL history. But at the time, no one was sure if he would be suspended for violating the league's NFL substance abuse policy, which he eventually was for two games. Moss was easily rated as the top wide receiver. One of these three players was sure to fall at number seven. But, now, the owner picking at number eight had a different choice. He could take Moss, but then not be guaranteed of getting a surefire running back. He could gamble on Lewis and the legal system. Or he could take another chance and select the 49ers' Kevan Barlow.

Every year there seems to be a wild card first-round pick. Barlow was that player in 2004. He didn't have first-round credentials, having split running back time with Garrison Hearst the previous two years. But Barlow's potential was mesmerizing. Here was a guy who rushed for 1,024 yards in 2003, averaging 5.1 yards a carry. Now he was going to be the 49ers' full-time runner in an offense where he figured to be the centerpiece. Barlow failed to meet expectations. The 49ers were the worst team in the league at 2-14—defenses keyed on Barlow, he got banged up, and he didn't catch many passes. In other words, Barlow wasn't worthy of being a number one pick.

Barlow was worth a shot in the second round. But he was just too unproven to take with your number one pick. Yes, it's a lot easier to make a decision when your choice is in the top seven. But even in the eighth to fourteenth range there are proven, reliable stars available. Unless an injury happens, you should always get steady, top-grade production from your number one pick. That's what a superstar provides.

STUD RUNNING BACK THEORY

Running backs are the key to fantasy success. So you want to get as many good ones as you can. That often means taking a running back with your first two draft picks and then grabbing a third and even fourth runner not many rounds later. Positions are not weighted equally in fantasy football, and running back is the most important position because of position scarcity.

From 1991 to 2005, the most dominant fantasy performer usually has been a running back. From 1991 through 1995, Emmitt Smith was the guy to get. During that five-year span Emmitt averaged 1,603 yards rushing and 17 touchdowns. Then Terrell Davis became the major fantasy force from 1996 through 1998. Davis was the Gale Sayers of his era, averaging 1,765 yards rushing and accounting for 53 touchdowns during this year three-period before a degenerative knee condition ended his career. Barry Sanders also added to the glamour of the position during that time. Sanders averaged 1,696 yards rushing during a five-year span from 1994-1998, but wasn't in Davis's fantasy class because he never scored more than 11 touchdowns in any of those seasons.

Colts rookie Edgerrin James burst on the fantasy scene in 1999 with 17 touchdowns, while also leading the league in rushing. James had a big fantasy season in 2000 too. But the dominant fantasy stud was Marshall Faulk. His all-purpose yardage and touchdowns were unmatched from 1998-2001. During this four-year period Faulk averaged 1,360 yards rushing, 887 yards receiving, and scored 69 touchdowns. Priest Holmes then took the torch as the number one fantasy player, averaging 1,530 yards rushing and 658 yards receiving from 2001-2003, while accounting for a phenomenal 61 touchdowns during this three-year period.

Shaun Alexander and LaDainian Tomlinson have a nice run going into the 2005 season. Alexander is the only player to score at least 14 rushing touchdowns each of the last four years. Tomlinson is averaging 1,474 yards rushing and 72 pass receptions during his first four seasons, scoring 60 touchdowns.

STUD QUARTERBACK THEORY

When using the **stud quarterback** theory, you rate the quarterback ahead of all other positions. It makes sense in leagues that are more quarterback-oriented, where touchdown passes count as much as rushing and receiving touchdowns, and passing yardage and completion figures weigh heavy in the scoring format. There are fewer "A" quarterbacks than "A" running backs. Even so, you must be convinced your quarterback can produce at least 30-35 touchdown passes and rank among the top three in passing yards to take him ahead of a running back or wide receiver.

There have been times when this theory has paid off. For example, in the 2004 season, Peyton Manning, Daunte Culpepper, and Donovan McNabb were the top fantasy-point scorers. All together, nine quarterbacks finished among the top sixteen in standard fantasy scoring leagues. The last time quarterbacks held such fantasy football dominance was 2001.

The top five fantasy point-producers in 2003 were running backs. Holmes, Tomlinson, Ahman Green, Jamal Lewis, and Clinton Portis led the way in a year in which seven of the top ten fantasy spots were running backs. Running backs also led the way in 2002, claiming eight of the top ten fantasy point places led by Holmes.

But in 2001, quarterbacks claimed nine of the first ten fantasy point places. Faulk was the only non-quarterback in the top ten. Kurt Warner had a sensational season, ranking Number 1 in fantasy production with 4,830 yards passing and 36 touchdowns. Quarterbacks also fared well in 2000, placing seventh among the top ten fantasy point scorers with Daunte Culpepper first and Jeff Garcia second.

TONY GONZALEZ TIGHT END THEORY

The **Tony Gonzalez tight end** theory is simply to get the premier stud tight end (if there is one) in leagues requiring a tight end—in particular, Chiefs tight end Tony Gonzalez. It has been a popular strategy ever since Gonzalez started dominating the position in 1999. Owners subscribing to this theory make it a priority to grab Gonzalez, even if they have to do it as early as late second round or early third round. Their thinking is that since Gonzalez usually is the lone stud at the position, it's a huge edge to have him. It's like starting an extra wide receiver when you have Gonzalez.

That strategy really paid off in 2000 when Gonzalez caught 93 passes for 1,203 yards and scored nine touchdowns. He was far ahead of the second-highest fantasy scoring tight end, Shannon Sharpe. What made this theory so popular was the scarcity of good tight ends.

However, in 2004 a number of star tight ends emerged. Gonzalez hauled in a tight end record 102 passes and outgained all other tight ends, but he didn't score the most touchdowns among tight ends, finishing with seven. Antonio Gates of the Chargers caught 13 touchdown passes, two more than Gonzalez ever caught in a season. Still, there were no complaints from Gonzalez owners.

WIDE RECEIVER THEORY

The **wide receiver** theory is based on the contrarian's viewpoint that if everybody is taking running backs and quarterbacks, then you should grab the best wide receivers. Those who go along with this theory believe it's wiser to take the top-rated receivers than the highest-ranked quarterbacks or running backs who fall outside of the top six. Often, these are owners who pick late in the first round and thus don't have the opportunity to grab the top running backs or quarterback. There really hasn't been a wide receiver worth considering as the top fantasy pick since Jerry Rice was in his prime in the mid- to late-1980s.

The wide receiver theory is a tough strategy to make work considering you not only need your wide receiver to stay healthy, but his quarterback as well. It's risky because you're banking on coming up with two competent starting running backs at some point in the draft. Most owners shy away from this theory, scared off by the lack of quality depth at running back.

But sometimes this theory accidentally comes into play with those picking early in the draft. They'll most likely take a franchise running back and then come back and take two of the five best receivers—one at the end of the second round and the other at the beginning of the third round—because they present the most value left on the board.

This theory makes more sense in leagues that award one point for each receiver reception. With teams figuring to throw more because of the increased emphasis on the illegal contact rule, the wide receiver theory is gaining more of a following. It is tempting to take Randy Moss with a late first round pick and then see Marvin Harrison, Terrell Owens, and Torry Holt available for your second round pick, with your other draft options being "B" level running backs and quarterbacks. Furthermore, this theory can be appealing because wide receivers get hurt less often than quarterbacks and running backs.

8. POSITIONS

RUNNING BACKS

You can win a fantasy championship with a mediocre quarterback or no dominant wide receivers. You can even win a fantasy championship without significant contributions from your tight end, kicker, or defense. But it's nearly impossible to win a championship without at least one stud running back.

Running back is the most important position in fantasy football. Not only do running backs score heavily in four categories—rushing yards, touchdowns, receptions, and receiving yards—but there is a scarcity of them compared to other positions. It comes down to supply and demand. There are not enough quality runners in leagues requiring two running back starters, which most leagues do.

Many leagues are composed of one quarterback, two running backs, two wide receivers, a tight end, kicker, defense, and flex position, where you can play either a wide receiver, tight end, or running back. With thirty-two NFL teams, there are more than enough for twelve teams to get a quality starting quarterback, decent tight end, solid defense, and respectable kicker.

There are enough wide receivers to go around, too, with most of the NFL teams having two good wide receivers. A few teams even have three wide receivers worth drafting. The Ravens, Browns, Bears, and 49ers were the only teams that didn't have at least one borderline starting fantasy wide receiver in 2004. You have a pool of fifty to sixty respectable wideouts to choose from each season.

It's a different story with running backs. Even in ten-team leagues, you still need twenty starting running backs. This doesn't even include the flex, or utility spot, which most owners like to fill with a running back. There just aren't twenty star runners available. In the last five years, there has been an average of eighteen solid running backs, half of which would be considered franchise runners. Running back scarcity is even more pronounced in twelve-owner leagues. The larger the league, the more important running backs become.

Some positions are easier to fill. Quarterbacks aren't a problem. There are about eighteen to twenty solid ones, who don't have to worry about losing their jobs. Wide receivers are the deepest position in fantasy football. There are fewer star tight ends, kickers, and defenses, but those are generally low-scoring positions in fantasy football. Running backs are what you have to worry about. Ideally, you want running backs who are going to get lots of touches. If a back carries the ball twenty-five times and has another half-dozen passes thrown his way, chances are he'll be putting up solid statistics regardless of his talent level. Heck, James Allen had a 1,000-yard rushing season in 2000 because the Bears fed him the ball 290 times.

Usually about one-fourth of the teams use a running back by committee approach, which impacts a running back's value. In 2004, no team had better running back depth than the Vikings with Onterrio Smith, Michael Bennett, Mewelde Moore, and Moe Williams. But the most rushing yards any of those talented backs gained was 544 yards. The Dolphins ended up trying four different runners in the featured role after Ricky Williams retired right before the start of the 2004 season. You really want to avoid backs on teams who use a platoon system. Their numbers are impacted, and it's frustrating to watch another back cut into what should be your team's carries. This puts even more emphasis on getting a heavy-duty back as soon as possible.

It's not such an accomplished feat anymore to rush for 1,000 yards in a season. All you need to do is average 62.5 yards per game. There were eighteen runners who did it in 2004 and also in 2003, with seventeen exceeding that figure in 2002. The average the past six years has been 17.6 runners finishing with more than 1,000 yards. Until the NFL lengthened the schedule to sixteen games, the average number of 1,000-yard rushers per year was fewer than three per season from 1934-1977.

Ideally you want to get that rare running back that is durable, consistent, runs for more than 1,500 yards, catches passes, and rings up a lot of touchdowns. Sounds nice, doesn't it? But there is only one LaDainian Tomlinson, Priest Holmes, Shaun Alexander, Clinton Portis, and Ahman Green to go around. These guys are the reason why there are such feeding frenzies to grab running backs early.

POSITIONS

If you miss out on Peyton Manning and Daunte Culpepper, you can fall back on a Trent Green, Brett Favre, Tom Brady, or Aaron Brooks to be your quarterback. Miss out on a franchise back with an early first-round pick, though, and you could be looking at a drop all the way to a Duce Staley, Warrick Dunn, and Michael Pittman by the time your second and third round picks come up. During a recent fourteen-team CBS SportsLine "experts" draft, for instance, eighteen of the first nineteen choices were running backs, with the first eleven all being runners.

Research shows us that there will probably be seventeen to eighteen runners who produce 1,000 yards each season. There hasn't been a repeat rushing leader going into 2005 since Edgerrin James in 1999 and 2000. The last to do it before James was Barry Sanders in 1996 and 1997. So don't feel you can't get a stud back if you miss out on the first eight. The trick is figuring out which ones to go after once the seemingly elite have been taken. Keep in mind, too, that running back is a high-reward, high-risk position. Fantasy seasons have been ruined by a superstar running back being knocked out for the season.

Only five starting running backs managed to play in every game during the 2004 season. Injuries are always a concern. It's one thing to replace a kicker, who you chose in the last round. It's another to come up with a substitute for a franchise back whose career was derailed by an injury like the careers of Terrell Davis, Jamal Anderson, and Bo Jackson were. Running backs get hit the most, taking not only a physical toll, but also a mental toll. Maybe that's why there is a higher chance of a running back suddenly retiring than other skill position players. Barry Sanders, Robert Smith, and Ricky Williams shocked a lot of people when they voluntarily quit in the prime of their careers. You can't ignore a running back's mental psyche.

Because of constant wear and tear, many running backs have a short shelf life. The pounding they take can cause them to flame out, seemingly overnight. Christian Okoye was a powerful hit for the Chiefs, leading the NFL in rushing in 1989. Three years later he was out of football. Jamal Anderson set an NFL record with 410 rushing attempts in 1998 while leading the league in rushing with 1,846 yards. But the following year, he suffered a serious knee injury with another only two years later, which finished his career.

What else should you look at when weighing which running back to choose? Talent obviously helps, but it's not the overriding factor. Being an integral part of the offense is huge. There were many younger backs that were better than an ancient Jerome Bettis in 2004. But the Steelers ran the ball a league-high 61 percent of the time. Because of that, Bettis, even though he started only about half the games, scored 13 touchdowns and ran for nearly 1,000 yards.

Having an offensive line that excels in run-blocking can turn backup running backs into studs as the Chiefs showed in 2004 when Derrick Blaylock and Larry Johnson filled in for Priest Holmes the last eight games. Blaylock and Johnson scored a combined 17 touchdowns while averaging 4.7 yards a carry. The Broncos' offensive line has helped produce a 1,000 yard rusher nine of the past ten years going into 2005, with five different rushers achieving the figure, including Olandis Gary, Mike Anderson, and Reuben Droughns.

Pass-catching skills come in handy in leagues rewarding receptions and receiving yards. For instance, not only did Tomlinson finish with the third most rushing yards in 2003, but he led the NFL in receptions, catching 100 passes. Not all backs, though, are sure-handed or do much in the passing game. Only once in Jamal Lewis's first four years has he caught more than 30 passes and had more than 300 yards receiving. Corey Dillon has been in the NFL eight years heading into 2005, and he's never had more than 300 receiving yards in a season. By comparison, Brian Westbrook was the number one receiving running back in 2004, topping 700 receiving yards and catching six touchdown passes. So don't just look at a back's rushing yardage figures when assessing his strengths and weaknesses.

If you are considering taking a rookie or second-year runner, find out if he can block well enough in pass protection. Some coaches are reluctant to play a young back full-time at the risk of his quarterback getting sacked. That was one of the factors that kept Kevan Barlow from being a full-time starter in San Francisco during the 2002 and 2003 seasons, despite respectively averaging 4.7 and 5.1 yards a carry.

Running backs are supposed to score touchdowns. That's another alluring thing about taking them high. But not all is fair in the yardage wars. Some backs like Bettis, Holmes, Alexander, and Tomlinson always seem to get a high share of touchdowns. But others can't. Some have bad luck like Edgerrin James did in 2004. James should have scored a lot more than nine rushing touchdowns with the Colts averaging 32.6 points a game, but Peyton Manning threw a record 49 touchdown passes.

Others don't get too many goal line touches. Warrick Dunn and Fred Taylor are prime examples of "B" runners who were pulled for goal line runners once their teams got inside the five-yard line. In terms of talent, Taylor is right there with any back. But he's accounted for just 10 touchdowns combined during the 2003 and 2004 seasons, so he can't be depended on to give you big points. Robert Smith is another case in point. Smith averaged 1,247 rushing yards a season during his final four years of 1997-2000. Yet he averaged only 5.2 touchdowns during that span because he rarely received any carries at the goal line. He never scored more than seven touchdowns a season.

Study the upside and downside of each back. Don't get sucked in by big names on the down side of their career. Runners begin slowing up once they reach the age of thirty. Curtis Martin was a rare exception in 2004, leading the league in rushing while having one of his finest seasons. That's not the norm, though. Running backs get old fast. Eddie George gained between 1,204 and 1,509 yards each of his first five years from 1996-2000.

However, in the next four years George never averaged more than 3.4 yards a carry. By reputation alone, Marshall Faulk was being picked in the second round during some 2004 drafts, even though he was thirty-one and it was clear from his subpar 2003 season he was slowing down. But these owners just remember the Faulk from 1999 to 2001, when he piled up 6,765 rushing and receiving yards and scored 59 touchdowns.

George and Faulk are easy to pick out as running backs whose skills have declined. Try to project who else might be slowing down because of wear and tear. Injuries often can be a telltale sign. Stephen Davis, Ahman Green, and Priest Holmes have mileage on them and all three were banged-up last year. On the opposite are young runners just coming into their own, like Willis McGahee, Kevin Jones, Julius Jones, and Steven Jackson. You might like a gifted back, but make sure he's not in a platoon rotation. I like DeShaun Foster, for instance, going into 2005, but he's never been in a full-time role before.

Foster suffered a broken collarbone just four weeks into the 2004 season that ended his year. Players coming back from an early-season injury who were just beginning to make an impression often get lost in the shuffle the following year, and can make good draft bargains.

Keep on top of any changes in offensive philosophy, because they can affect a runner in a positive or negative manner. Deuce McAllister had a down season in 2004, and it wasn't entirely because he suffered a high ankle sprain. McAllister was used to having a fullback as his lead blocker. But the Saints switched away from that formation. McAllister wasn't as comfortable and didn't like it. Clinton Portis had a tough time, too, picking up the pounding, in-between-the-tackles running style of Joe Gibbs after being traded to the Redskins from the Broncos. The smallish Portis scored 29 touchdowns in 29 games for the Broncos while averaging 5.5 yards a carry. But with the Redskins, he scored just five touchdowns and averaged only 3.8 yards per attempt.

Some runners thrive when a new coach or system is put into place. Faulk became the most dominant fantasy player for three years after he was traded to the Rams. Jamal Anderson was a one-man show for the Falcons until he was felled by a knee injury. Holmes averaged less than 550 yards rushing and scored a total of three touchdowns his last two years with the Ravens in 1999 and 2000 before busting out with the Chiefs when he became their featured back.

QUARTERBACKS

As important as the position is in real football, quarterback just isn't as valuable in fantasy football. There are just too many solid quarterbacks and not enough running backs and dominant wide receivers. At least, that's been the prevalent belief for many years. However, following the 2004 season, that thinking is now open to debate. After seeing how officials are enforcing the illegal contact rule, and digesting the mind-boggling numbers Peyton Manning and Daunte Culpepper put up in 2004, fantasy owners are rethinking if they should indeed use a high draft pick to take their quarterback.

Conventional thinking is that quarterback has always been the easiest position to fill in a fantasy league, and the statistics back it up. There have been at least ten quarterbacks who threw for 20 or more touchdowns in seven of the past eight years. In each of the past five years, there have been at least eight quarterbacks who passed for more than 3,500 yards.

Why use your number one or number two draft choice on a quarterback when you could wait for the middle rounds and still get Brett Favre, Trent Green, Tom Brady, Chad Pennington, Steve McNair, Drew Brees, Aaron Brooks, Jake Delhomme, Marc Bulger, or Matt Hasselbeck? Favre always seems to drift in drafts, yet he was the only quarterback to throw for more than 29 touchdowns in 2003. There were 30 or more touchdown passes thrown thirteen times in a seven-year span from 1997-2003. That averages fewer than two quarterbacks a year achieving the magic 30-touchdown mark. No quarterback threw for 30 or more touchdowns in 2002. While that makes Manning and Culpepper's 2004 achievements all the more impressive, it does draw attention to how bunched up the position is.

Many owners bypass their quarterback spot, loading up on running backs and wide receivers before getting a safe "B" quarterback in the middle rounds. But Manning, with his NFL-record 49 touchdown passes, 121.3 rating, and 4,557 yards passing in 2004, taught us to respect the quarterback position again. How good are those numbers in fantasy terms? Using a standard fantasy league scoring system of four points for a passing touchdown and six points for a rushing or receiving score, Manning's touchdown figure is the equivalent of a running back or wide receiver putting up 33 touchdowns. If touchdown passes are weighed equally with rushing and receiving touchdowns, Manning then had 49 scores. That's more than double the rushing record for touchdowns in a season of 27 set by Priest Holmes in 2003. Manning single-handedly won fantasy titles for his owners. This was only done one other time in recent memory by a quarterback in fantasy football—Kurt Warner in 1999, when he threw for 41 touchdowns. It is doubtful many people were playing fantasy football in 1984 and 1986 when Dan Marino threw 48 and 44 touchdowns, respectively.

Manning has everything going to put up historic numbers with three outstanding wide receivers, two good pass-catching tight ends, excellent pass protection, and a domed stadium in which to play. But it wasn't just Manning in 2004. There were other quarterbacks, who if it weren't for Manning, would be attracting far more attention for the statistics they compiled. Daunte Culpepper had 39 touchdown passes, the fifth-most in NFL history, and threw for more yards than even Manning. Culpepper achieved this without having Randy Moss for five games.

Donovan McNabb moved into first-round consideration accounting for 34 touchdowns and nearly 4,000 yards, despite throwing only three passes the last two weeks of the season because the Eagles had already clinched home-field advantage for the playoffs. Trent Green threw 27 touchdown passes and had 4,591 yards passing, the second straight season he surpassed 4,000 yards. Just two years ago, Green would have finished second in both yardage and touchdown passes with those figures. Even the much maligned Jake Plummer threw for more than 4,000 yards, breaking John Elway's Broncos record. Plummer threw 27 touchdowns, tying Elway's team mark.

There were five quarterbacks going above the 4,000 mark in 2004. (Favre reached that figure, too.) The last time five quarterbacks surpassed 4,000 yards was in 1999. In the four years from 2000 to 2003, the 4,000 passing yardage figure was exceeded just eleven times. Warner and Manning were the only ones reaching 4,000 in 2001. In 2002, Manning, Rich Gannon, Drew Bledsoe, and Kerry Collins hit the 4,000 passing yardage mark. Only Manning and Green, though, threw for 4,000 yards in 2003.

It has become obvious the NFL achieved its goal of increasing offense by having officials stress the illegal contact rule. The look-but-don't-touch rules for defenders opened up the passing game. Scoring increased from an average of 41 points a game in 2003 to 43 points in 2004, and yards per completion was up from 11.2 to 11.8, as there were 43 more illegal contact penalties called from 2003 to 2004. Passing touchdowns were up to an average of 1.4 a game after being either at 1.2 or 1.3 the previous four years.

Certainly Manning and Culpepper, both in their prime entering the 2005 season, have proven without a doubt they are worthy of being taken with a high draft pick. It has reached the point with these two that it is debatable if they should be taken first or second overall ahead of any running back. That kind of talk used to be sacrilegious with everyone pushing running backs so strongly. Still, let's not allow ourselves to get too caught up in this quarterback euphoria. There's a drop-off after Manning, Culpepper, and McNabb.

These three did a lot to camouflage some of the more mundane and less appealing aspects of the position. Don't forget that quarterbacks are more susceptible to injury. Nearly half of the teams in the NFL lost their starting quarterback to injury for at least one game during the 2004 season. On average, fifty-five to sixty different starting quarterbacks have been used during the course of a season over the past seven years. The only starting quarterbacks from 2004 who hadn't missed some games during their careers because of injury are Favre, Brady, Manning, Brooks, Delhomme, and Drew Brees.

It's not just injuries. Quarterbacks can be a scapegoat when offenses don't click. Cardinals Coach Dennis Green made three quarterback changes alone during a three-week span in 2004. This is a risk you take if you wait too long to draft a quarterback, and a real danger if you end up with a lower echelon quarterback. Sometimes even "B" quarterbacks can get the hook. That's what happened to Bucs' quarterback Brad Johnson after four games of the 2004 season. There have been more than forty quarterback switches not related to injury during the past two years.

Quarterback is a fickle position. With rare exceptions like Ben Roethlisberger, it usually takes several years for a quarterback to reach maturity. It's not easy for a young quarterback to immediately adjust to the speed of the game at the pro level, understand the complexities involved, learn a new philosophy, get comfortable with teammates, and figure out defensive schemes. As good as Roethlisberger was during his rookie year of 2004, he was far from being an elite fantasy quarterback. There were eighteen quarterbacks who threw more touchdowns than Roethlisberger and twenty-one who passed for more yards. You're better off going with a late-bloomer than a rookie quarterback. The success rate is higher for these types, who bounced from team to team in the NFL, sometimes having learned their craft in the CFL or Arena Football League. Examples include Rich Gannon, Jeff Garcia, Brad Johnson, Warren Moon, Tommy Maddox, and Kurt Warner. Brees surprised a lot of people during 2004, finishing with the third highest quarterback rating behind Manning and Culpepper, while tossing 27 touchdown passes. But Brees was in his fourth season.

Sometimes things just click with a quarterback. He can get into the perfect system for his style and things take off. This was the case with Warner when he started for the Rams. In other instances, a quarterback and head coach make a good fit such as journeyman Vinny Testaverde and Bill Parcells in 2000 with the Jets. Up until 2004, the average age of the starting quarterback for the final eight playoff teams was 29.8 years. That's going back to 1990. It is expecting too much for a young quarterback to make much of a fantasy impact early in his career, as those experiencing Eli Manning in 2004 could tell you.

Keep in perspective, too, that while scoring picked up in 2004 and the number of touchdown passes increased to 732, which was 77 more than the previous four-year average of 654 per season compiled from 2000 to 2003, passing yards actually decreased four of the past five seasons.

Passing yards per game was 210 in 2004. In 2003 it was 214 yards. This was up two yards from 2002, but down from 2001 and 2000. Quarterbacks averaged 222 yards in 2000 and 220 yards in 2001. Some of this low average in 2004 can be explained by the vertically challenged Bears, who averaged a high school figure of just 137 yards passing. The Ravens weren't a whole lot better, putting up only 144 yards per game.

I can't fault anyone who takes Peyton Manning and Culpepper with a top-five pick coming off their great 2004 seasons. Culpepper might even be the better choice when you factor in his 406 rushing yards. All together, he accounted for 5,123 passing and rushing yards for the Vikings along with 41 touchdowns. There's no reason why Manning and Culpepper can't continue to put up astounding numbers. Figuring Terrell Owens returns healthy, McNabb could be worth a first-round investment, too.

It was running backs, not quarterbacks, who actually suffered more injuries in 2004 as first- or second-round picks Priest Holmes, Jamal Lewis, Deuce McAllister, Stephen Davis, Travis Henry, Domanick Davis, Duce Staley, Chris Brown, Thomas Jones, and Kevin Barlow all missed at least one game because of injury. By contrast, the only significant quarterback injuries were to Steve McNair, Rich Gannon, Rex Grossman, and Tim Rattay. Historically, though, quarterback is the position hardest hit.

After the Big Three of Manning, Culpepper, and McNabb go, there could be a lull before the next quarterback is picked. Somebody will probably risk a high pick on the ever-intriguing Michael Vick. But after him, there's no rush. There's a solid "B" core of Tom Brady, Drew Brees, Chad Pennington, Jake Plummer, Trent Green, Aaron Brooks, Brett Favre, Marc Bulger, Matt Hasselbeck, and Kerry Collins. These guys are all good but have one or two negatives. Still, this gives you a total of fourteen "B" quarterbacks or better. So there's plenty to go around.

The next tier—the "C" group of quarterbacks—is a mixture of guys with potential who may or may not have breakout seasons—veterans who could lose their starting status at some point and unproven young quarterbacks. In fantasy leagues requiring just one starting quarterback, these "C" players would serve as backups and possible spot starters.

If your league mandates you to start two or more quarterbacks, and has a lot of owners, you may have to dip into the "D" group. This group includes the disappointments and those in an unsettled starting role. The "F" list is composed of second-string quarterbacks who may or may not get a shot at playing.

Talent and statistics shouldn't be your only criteria in choosing your quarterbacks. Don't forget to take into account the quality of receivers, if the team throws a lot, what kind of offense they run, their schedule, whether they are in an easy or hard division, and if that quarterback has any competition behind him where there's a chance he could lose his job. Roethlisberger's fantasy numbers were hurt in 2004, for instance, because the Steelers ran the ball a league-high 61 percent of the time. The Steelers passed an NFL-low 358 times in 2004. By contrast, the league average was 511 pass attempts per team. Culpepper and Favre's numbers, on the other hand, were helped because they got to throw against three weak secondaries in their NFC North division. It was similar with Brees, operating in his AFC West division against the Raiders and Chiefs, who ranked thirtieth and thirty-first defensively in 2004.

It would be nice to have Peyton Manning or Culpepper going for you, but any of the "B" quarterbacks can lead you to a fantasy title, too, when coupled with a franchise running back and a pair of upper tier wide receivers. If you miss out on any of the "A" and "B" quarterbacks, better make sure to take two or three of the "C" quarterbacks. In that case, you're really going to have to play matchups, where you pick your quarterback based on the opponent and situation.

WIDE RECEIVERS

Maybe the biggest surprise of the 2004 fantasy season was Carolina's Muhsin Muhammad leading all receivers in yardage and touchdowns. Muhammad wasn't even rated in the top forty-five by some owners and publications. He went undrafted in leagues. Perhaps it shouldn't have been such big shock, because of all the positions, wide receivers are the most puzzling. You generally know what you're getting with a running back and quarterback. But wide receivers are more of an enigma. Their statistics depend on who is throwing to them and the type of offense they're in.

In terms of talent, the Dolphins' Chris Chambers takes a backseat to few. But Chambers has been prevented from becoming a stud fantasy player because of the Dolphins' conservative nature and below average quarterbacks. The four best wide receivers the past few years, Randy Moss, Marvin Harrison, Torry Holt, and Terrell Owens, all played with good quarterbacks and are in systems that maximize their high skill level. These four remain in the highest echelon. They are the no-brain picks with Moss and Owens strong enough to take in the first round. But what makes wide receiver the trickiest position is coming up with the right "B" and "C" wide receivers. Many leagues require you to start three wide receivers, plus a flex spot that can also be filled with a wide receiver. So you need to go deep into the position.

The landscape can change fast, either up or down, when it comes to wide receivers. Muhammad had been a dependable, but mundane wideout going into 2004. He had averaged 748 yards the past three years, scoring a total of seven touchdowns from 2001 to 2003. His last big year was 2000. The Carolina receiver fantasy owners were targeting was Steve Smith. There wasn't too much enthusiasm for Muhammad, who seemed to be over-the-hill, was playing on a ball-control running offense and with a still largely unproven quarterback in Jake Delhomme.

So what happened? Smith suffered a broken leg in the opening game that knocked him out for the season. The Panthers lost their top five running backs, forcing them to become a passing team and Delhomme proved to be a solid quarterback. Presto—Muhammad turned into a fantasy monster, finishing with 1,405 receiving yards and 16 touchdowns.

Find the right wide receivers in the middle rounds to go with a stud running back and solid quarterback and you have a formula that can win your league title. That's why rounds three to seven are littered with receivers being picked. This is when the second tier, or "B," receivers fall. There are "B plus" receivers like Chad Johnson, Javon Walker, Hines Ward, Andre Johnson, and Joe Horn who earned their mark by consistency in Ward and Horn's cases, or have a high ceiling where their already outstanding numbers could keep getting better as in the case of Walker, Chad Johnson, and Andre Johnson. There are a number of standard "B" receivers, too, such as Darrell Jackson, Santana Moss, Eric Moulds, Chris Chambers, Reggie Wayne, Jimmy Smith, Derrick Mason, Rod Smith, Jerry Porter, Laveranues Coles, and Isaac Bruce.

The "B minus" list has good receivers as well. Some coming off injuries like Charles Rogers and Steve Smith, some having to prove their rookie years weren't a fluke like Michael Clayton and Roy Williams, and some being a number three wideout on a great passing team like Brandon Stokley. There are others who have to show more consistency like Eddie Kennison, and others downgraded for their team's weak quarterbacking like Keyshawn Johnson, Anquan Boldin, and Larry Fitzgerald. That's what makes them B minuses.

Usually when quarterbacks and running backs gain a lot of yardage it translates into touchdowns for them. That's not always so with wide receivers. Moss, Owens, Harrison, and Chad Johnson get their touchdowns. But it's not always a given for many others. Holt, for example, led the NFL in receiving yards in 2000, but he scored just six touchdowns. Moss was the only wide receiver to score more than 12 touchdowns in 2003. Only four wide receivers had double-digit touchdowns in 2002. Harrison finished eighteenth in receiving yards in 2004, but scored 15 touchdowns. Isaac Bruce, by contrast, finished fifth in receiving yards, yet reached the end zone just six times.

Receivers can age rapidly. That's what happened to Antonio Freeman. He had six good years with the Packers from 1996-2001, but then lost a step and turned into a journeyman. Sometimes an injury can slow them down to the point where they lose their effectiveness. That's what happened to Herman Moore, who led the NFL in receptions in 1997 and to Marcus Robinson, Germane Crowell, and Michael Westbrook, all of whom placed in the top ten in receiving yards in 1999.

With the exception of Moss, it's rare to find a rookie receiver having a major impact. There wasn't a rookie wide receiver that caught more than 50 passes in 2002, and only two who reached that figure in 2003. In the 2004 NFL draft, seven wide receivers were selected in the first round. Clayton was the only one to catch more than 58 passes and gain more than 850 yards his rookie season, although Williams, Fitzgerald, and Lee Evans all displayed excellent potential. There have been 316 wide receivers drafted since 1995. Guess how many exceeded 1,000 yards their rookie season? The grand total is five—Joey Galloway in 1995 with Seattle, Terry Glenn in 1996 with New England, Moss in 1998 with Minnesota, Anquan Boldin in 2003 with Arizona, and Clayton with Tampa

Bay in 2004. Moss is the only one to have more than eight touchdowns his first season.

Astute owners like to grab wide receivers beginning their third season. That seems to be the breakout year for receivers because by then they have had a chance to mature, adjust to quicker, physical NFL secondaries, and learn their quarterback while getting their timing and rhythm down.

The Packers' Walker was in his third year when he finished third in receiving yards with 1,382 and scored 12 touchdowns in 2004. Ashley Lelie played much better during his third season in 2004 as well, averaging an NFL-high 20.1 yards a reception. They are not the only examples. In 1999 Holt, David Boston, Peerless Price, and Marty Booker were all rookies. Here are their comparisons from their first year and their third season: Holt increased his yardage from 788 to 1,363 in his third season, Boston went from 473 his rookie year to a league-leading 1,598 his third year, Price had a 502-yard increase from 393 to 895, while Booker went from 219 to 1,071.

The following year Plaxico Burress, Todd Pinkston, Jerry Porter, and Coles all were rookies. Burress had 273 receiving yards his rookie year in 2000. He had 1,325 in 2003. Pinkston increased his receiving yards from 181 to 798. Porter went from just six yards to 688 and nine touchdowns, while Coles went from 370 to 1,264. The nice thing is often you can get these third-year breakout wide receivers late in the draft because their statistics haven't blossomed yet and there isn't a big demand for them.

You would think there would be more emphasis on the passing game because of stricter enforcement of the rules regulating holding, bumping, and grabbing receivers once they get more than five yards downfield. Some teams didn't take full advantage of this rule interpretation in 2004. Surprisingly, pass attempts were down to 16,354 from 16,493 in 2003 and 17,292 in 2002.

That should change this season as teams have had a year to study and digest how best to take advantage of the situation. This statistic also is skewed because of the Steelers, who threw only 358 passes in 2004. The next lowest passing team was the Falcons, who threw 395 times. If you don't include the Steelers' passing attempts, the other thirty-one teams averaged 516 attempts. That's one more than NFL teams averaged in 2003.

This makes wide receivers even more valuable, especially in leagues that factor in receptions, not just yards and touchdowns. While I'm not radical enough to suggest taking wide receivers with your top three picks, I certainly wouldn't denigrate an owner for coming away with two wide receivers in the first three rounds. I could perfectly understand, too, an owner even taking three pass catchers during the first four rounds in leagues where each wide receiver/tight end reception counts one point and running back receptions count as a half point. This would apply in standard yardage type leagues where you receive one point for every 10 yards receiving as opposed to one point for every 25 yards rushing.

There is more quality depth at wide receiver than any other fantasy position. Because of that, some owners don't feel a compelling urge to get their top receivers right away. This is understandable, especially in leagues where touchdowns count the most. There has been a drop-off in fantasy points from the top five receivers to the next tier during the past five years. Unlike other positions, there is also more open debate in ranking the top receivers once you get past Moss, Owens, Harrison, and Holt.

There is no strong consensus like there usually is at running back. Moss and Owens still had big touchdown seasons in 2004 despite suffering injuries that cost Moss five games and Owens two games. They still combined for 27 touchdowns. If you add Harrison's 15 touchdowns and Holt's 10 scores, that accounts for 52 of the 732 touchdown receptions, which is 14 percent of the receiving touchdowns scored in 2004.

Everybody knows about these guys, though. It's who you get at your number two and number three wide receiving spots that can propel you to your league title. Owners who projected Manning and the Colts to be a passing machine and hopped on Reggie Wayne and Brandon Stokley were rewarded when those two respectively finished ninth and twenty-first in receiving yardage, while combining to put up 22 touchdowns. There are surprises every year at wide receiver. That's why it's important to take a few shots late in your draft on wide receivers.

Look for guys who are finally getting a full-time chance. It can be because of an injury, trade or free agency—really anything that changes their circumstances. It's all about opportunity. Drew Bennett is an example from 2004. He moved into the Titans' starting lineup after the team traded Justin McCareins to the Jets. Bennett is also an illustration of a receiver whose numbers can rise considerably when a team loses their best running back, has a bad defense, and is forced to pass a lot. That's what happened to the Titans down the stretch in 2004. Bennett was the prime beneficiary hauling in 28 passes for 517 yards and scoring eight touchdowns during Weeks 13-15. The Titans surrendered 140 points during that three-week span.

With all the information available, some owners get too caught up taking young receivers instead of proven veterans because they believe the jackpot could be more rewarding. They get more of an adrenalin rush gambling on high-risk, potential high-reward receivers. They downgrade reliable stars like Isaac Bruce, Jimmy Smith, Rod Smith, Eric Moulds, and Keyshawn Johnson because they aren't young anymore and have lost some speed. You need dependable receivers, though. Those five veterans all happened to finish among the top twenty-five wide receivers in receiving yardage for 2004. A flashy wide receiver that has a great game once every four weeks isn't going to win you many head-to-head league titles. Consistency from week to week is imperative.

There's nothing wrong with taking a young wide receiver, if he has an upside and is in a promising situation. A good situation means a team that has a decent offense and a wide receiver opening. The Vikings were looking for a number two wide receiver to go alongside Moss in 2004. Nate Burleson emerged, putting up more than 1,000 receiving yards and scoring nine touchdowns. The Bengals needed to replace injured Peter Warrick and his

79 catches from 2003. Up stepped T. J. Houshmandzadeh. He caught 73 balls for 978 yards. You could have gotten Burleson and Houshmandzadeh in the last round of your 2004 draft.

Patience, however, is often required. You can't expect instant production. If your draft doesn't go enough rounds where you can stockpile extra wide receivers, don't throw away your notes. Keep an eye on these under-the-radar wide receivers and when they start getting the chance, be ready to make a free agency pickup. Michael Clayton didn't become a legitimate starting fantasy wide receiver until Week 4, and Houshmandzadeh didn't become a factor until Week 12. Burleson scored six of his nine touchdowns the last eight weeks of the season.

Having good wide receiver depth allows you to play matchups, where you can game-plan according to the defense, situation, and weather elements your players are up against that week. You never want to bench your best wide receivers no matter how dubious the matchup appears on paper. I made that mistake in Week 10 of the 2004 season. For the first and only time that season I benched Chad Johnson. It was strictly a match-up decision that caused me to sit out my best receiver. The Bengals were on the road against the Ravens with their fierce defense and Pro Bowl cornerback Chris McAlister. I was nauseous after seeing Johnson catch 10 passes for 162 yards and score two touchdowns against the Ravens. If your bench contains enough good receiver options, then you have the flexibility to mix and match your number three wideout and flex position each week. This flexibility comes in handy during the bye week period.

TIGHT ENDS

With the exception of Tony Gonzalez and Shannon Sharpe, tight end has been a positional graveyard for fantasy football owners through the years. The tight end landscape was so barren, some leagues actually eliminated the position, grouping tight ends with wide receivers. There were only three or four tight ends worth taking. All that changed, though, in 2004. Suddenly tight end became a hot position, with no other area making a bigger leap in production. Owners who had taken certain unsung tight ends as an afterthought late in their draft were winning titles. Forget Bill Gates—Antonio Gates brings the wealth when it comes to fantasy football.

Only twelve tight ends led their club in receiving in the five-year span from 1999 to 2003, and only four had topped their team in receiving during the 2002-2004 seasons. The lid was blown off in 2004 as eight tight ends finished number one on their team in passes caught. That's one-fourth of the NFL teams, and this doesn't include the Ravens' Todd Heap. He finished eight receptions behind the club leader despite missing nine games. Just recently, in 2002, no tight end led his team in receiving.

Gonzalez was the only tight end to lead his club in receiving during 2003. Gonzalez was his usual dominating presence in 2004, hauling in an NFL-record 102 passes for a tight end, 40 more than his next closest Chiefs teammate.

This time Gonzalez wasn't alone in holding up the position. Gates broke a Chargers team touchdown mark and NFL tight end record by scoring thirteen times in

2004, while catching 28 more throws than his next closest teammate. The 49ers' Eric Johnson had 35 more receptions than his closest pursuer on the 49ers. Jason Witten set a Cowboys tight end record, hauling in 87 passes. The Dolphins' Randy McMichael, Vikings' Jermaine Wiggins, Falcons' Alge Crumpler, and Giants' Jeremy Shockey all led their respective clubs in receptions in 2004.

There were nineteen tight ends that scored four or more touchdowns, compared to eight who managed to reach that figure in 2003. This trend might have been even higher if heralded rookie Kellen Winslow Jr. hadn't suffered a season-ending broken leg during the second game of the year, and if Heap would have been healthier.

Many of these tight ends like Gates, Witten, Johnson, Daniel Graham (who scored seven touchdowns), and promising Redskins rookie Chris Cooley weren't picked until late in fantasy drafts or plucked from the free agent pool. Gonzalez, Witten, Gates, and Johnson all finished in the top thirty-five in receiving yardage. Gonzalez placed seventh with 1,258 yards, only the second time since 1997 that a tight end finished in the top ten in receiving yards.

This tight end Renaissance came out of nowhere. It actually seemed 2004 would be another down year for tight ends with such dependable ones as Sharpe, Wesley Walls, and Frank Wycheck all calling it quits before the season. With the exception of Ben Coates, who from 1993-1998 scored 44 touchdowns and averaged 805 receiving yards, it seemed that Sharpe and Walls were about the only tight ends worth owning during the last ten to twelve years. The last great period for tight ends was the Jurassic era when Todd Christensen, Kellen Winslow Sr., and Ozzie Newsome finished 1-2-3 in receptions in 1983.

So is this just an aberration that happens every twenty years with tight ends, or is this a serious rebirth of the position? I think it might be a combination of the two. Tight ends have been helped by defenses playing more "cover 2" zones, which leave the middle of the field open while guarding the flanks against speedy wide receivers. Defenses will soon learn to adapt, evolve, and change if they become vulnerable to tight ends. I see a lot more coaches tailoring their defense to slow down Gates and not just concentrate all the time on stopping LaDainian Tomlinson.

The NFL's increased emphasis on calling defensive holding and pass interference had a trickle down effect on tight ends. They were beneficiaries as much as quarterbacks and wide receivers. Tight ends were able to get more isolated in 2004 against a linebacker or safety. This created a nice mismatch in speed, size, or both. Defenses will gradually adjust—they always do.

Yet, on the other hand, don't look for a shortage of talented tight ends. College football teams are passing more and utilizing tight ends. Many programs aren't just using their tight end to block. Today's athlete is bigger, more athletic, and has more speed. It takes a great all-around athlete to be a pass-catching tight end as Winslow, Gates, and Gonzalez have shown. They have made tight end a glamour position.

College players covet the position now, knowing the pros are placing more of an emphasis on it. Kellen Winslow Jr. was the sixth overall pick in the 2004 draft. Ben

Watson also was a first-round pick in 2004. Heath Miller was a first-round choice in 2005. Dallas Clark, Daniel Graham, Shockey, and Heap all were first-round picks in either 2001, 2002, or 2003. They weren't selected just so they could go out and tie up the strongside linebacker. NFL coaches have come to realize the full value of having a dangerous pass-catching tight end with speed and athleticism.

Some tight ends even flank out on the line of scrimmage like wide receivers. In this day and age, it is fullbacks who are used the way tight ends used to be employed. It's the fullbacks who block nearly every play, stopping once in a while to catch a short pass. Rarely do they get to carry the ball anymore. Nowadays it's much more fun for a fantasy owner to shop for a tight end. No more holding the nose and saying the words, "Andrew Glover," during the last round of your draft, or taking wasted shots on failed sleepers like O. J. Santiago, or being perennially disappointed by choosing Ricky Dudley or taking Eric Green too high every season. Those days are thankfully, and hopefully everlastingly, gone.

For the first time, you don't have to fight off anxiety attacks and nausea if you don't land Gonzalez, Gates, Crumpler, or Heap in your draft. Gates joins Gonzalez as a premier player at the position. Both are solid third-round picks. Some owners might even jump the gun and take them as high as late second round.

Getting Gonzalez has been a cornerstone strategy of some owners. An owner who won my head-to-head league in 2004 said taking Gonzalez in the third round was his biggest key. However, I'm not big on taking a tight end that high. Gates had a magical 2004 season, and won't be such a secret to defenses in 2005. They'll adjust and center more of their attention on him.

I've always taken my tight end late in the draft, and admittedly often paid the price for it in low production. I've tried veterans like Freddie Jones, over-the-hill, one-time-dangerous tight ends like Jackie Harris, players anticipated to have big roles on their team but didn't, like Desmond Clark and sleepers like Tyrone Davis. I never had much sustained success. But there couldn't be a better time to try this method than at a time when the tight end crop is the deepest and most talented it has ever been. There's plenty to go around in ten-owner leagues. Even in fourteen-team leagues you shouldn't get stuck with a stiff.

Gonzalez and Gates are going high. Then there will be a lull as far as tight ends being picked. But once teams have their quarterback, two running backs, and two wide receivers, you'll see "B" tight ends snatched up, such as Crumpler, Shockey, Witten, Heap, and McMichael. Eric Johnson might go around this time, too, depending on how the 49ers decide to fix their ruins.

Don't worry if you miss out on this batch. There's still plenty left. Unlike previous seasons, you can wait all the way to the last round and come away with a tight end you can be proud of. There's Bubba Franks, a reliable choice in leagues with a strong emphasis on touchdowns, as well as the promising Dallas Clark and Chris Cooley. The Vikings have a history of going a lot to their tight end, which could mean either Wiggins or Jim Kleinsasser, who played just one game in 2004 before suffering a season-ending broken leg. Graham still remains intriguing.

There will be tight ends people forget about because they disappointed in 2004, like Boo Williams and Desmond Clark. There also will be young tight ends available who are poised for big years, guys like Ben Troupe and L. J. Smith. So there's no reason anymore to sweat out your tight end. If Gonzalez or Gates happen to drop to the mid- to late-fourth round, they won't get past me. I would take one of them there.

With so many good tight ends, I wouldn't have much interest in taking one of the "B" ones in the middle rounds unless Heap happens to keep slipping. I have no problem waiting until the final round to get my tight end, and I still find a lot of nice options available. I'm more confident that this is the route to take than ever before.

DEFENSE

Having a great defense is vital to NFL teams, but it's not that important in fantasy football. This doesn't mean that you should forget about the position. You just don't have to place a high priority on it. There have been years when I didn't draft defense until the final round.

What's the point? So many defenses don't live up to preseason hype or follow the previous year's statistics. Injuries and free agent defections can change a defense overnight. Offenses have become so potent, especially now with the increased emphasis on defensive pass inter-ference, that defensive statistics don't often play a signifi-cant part in your fantasy football tally for the week.

Take scoring. Many fantasy leagues give you six points for a shutout and three if your defense holds a team under ten points. How many times does that happen? There were only four shutouts in 2004. The average number of shutouts in the five years from 2000-2004 was eight per season. That's eight in 512 regular season games—less than 2 percent.

In many leagues you can also score points on defense from sacks, fumble recoveries, interceptions, and special team touchdowns. Sacks and turnovers usually count for just one point, so it takes a lot of them to really add up. Defensive touchdowns and special team scores count six points, but rarely occur.

Let's say the defense you're using holds the opposition to thirteen points, intercepts two passes, recovers a fumble, and comes up with four sacks. That's a pretty strong effort, wouldn't you say? Sure, by NFL standards. But fantasy-wise it would account for just seven points using a traditional scoring system.

Since the opposition scored more than ten points, your defense wouldn't get any points there. Your defense would get two points for the two interceptions, one point for the fumble recovery, and four points for the four sacks. A wide receiver exceeds that just by catching a 10-yard touchdown pass. The wide receiver would get six points for the touchdown, one point for the reception, and one point for every 10 receiving yards. Thus he scores a total of eight points with just that one pass caught.

Still want to take a defense high in the draft? Some owners do. They might take a defense before the ninth round, which is too early in my view. An "A" defense isn't the same as taking an "A" position player. There is too much randomness involved with defenses compared to elite quarterbacks, running backs, and wide receivers. Many times the top two defenses selected don't live up to expectations. They tend to be overrated and overhyped. The Buccaneers were the number one defense going into 2003 drafts after allowing the fewest points and yards in 2002. The Bucs tumbled to tenth in defense during 2003 and finished twenty-second in 2004.

The Bills were the top producing fantasy defense in 2004. The Bills' defense wasn't even drafted in some leagues, because the Bills had the fewest takeaways in the league during the 2002 and 2003 seasons. I took the Patriots' defense in the tenth round of my head-to-head league, the earliest I'd ever selected a defense. The Patriots shut out three teams in 2003. But they didn't hold any team scoreless in 2004, were hit by a cluster injury problem in their secondary, and finished ninth overall in team defense.

Injuries can ruin a defense. Sometimes it can be a cluster injury problem that does in a defense, or sometimes it can just be the loss of one key individual. The Titans led the NFL in rush defense in 2003, but allowed the third-most points in the NFL the following season when they suffered multiple injuries at linebacker and in the secondary. The Bears' defense wasn't the same in 2004 when star linebacker Brian Urlacher was out. Urlacher missed seven games in 2004 because of assorted aliments. In those games the Bears allowed an average of 26 points. In the nine games Urlacher played, the Bears surrendered an average of 16.5 points.

Take a look, too, at special teams when thinking about your defense. The Bills had a combined five punt and kickoff returns for touchdowns. Those count for your defense. There are teams like the Panthers who are perennially strong in the special teams department. While you can't predict special teams touchdowns, be aware of who the dangerous returners are. Dante Hall single-handedly made the Chiefs defense a fantasy consideration by returning kicks for touchdowns an NFL-record four straight weeks during the 2003 season. Allen Rossum, Eddie Drummond, Michael Lewis, Jerry Azumah, and Antwaan Randle El are other feared kick and punt returners. Brian Mitchell made the Redskins defense and later the Eagles defense more attractive for fantasy players from 1991 to 2002 returning nine kicks and punts for touchdowns during that span.

But don't take your defense solely based on a team having an excellent return man. There were only twenty-six combined punt/kickoff return touchdowns in 2004. Treat returners as just an added plus or minus when assessing defenses. Don't make them your determining factor. Mitchell, the NFL's career leader in return yardage, never had more than two return touchdowns in a season. Hall followed his great 2003 season with no punt return touchdowns, although he did bring back two kickoffs for scores.

Team Defense Strategy

One popular defensive strategy is to draft two defenses, then start the one that has the better matchup for the week. This is called **matchup strategy** and can work well. Depending on your league structure, and your available bench space, you may be able to take three or four defenses. At least one of your defenses should have a favorable matchup that week. If you're using this matchup strategy, though, you need to take into consideration various factors. Ideally you'd like to pit your defense against a struggling offense.

Defenses usually play better at home. So home-field is important. Going against an inexperienced quarterback at home often works, like the Lions did during Week 13 of the 2004 season against Cardinals' rookie quarterback John Navarre. The Lions weren't even a top-twenty defense, but they made a great play that week because of these circumstances. Navarre, a rookie seventh-round draft pick making his first start, was 18 for 40 and threw four interceptions. As expected, he was totally overmatched. Because of injuries to their first two quarterbacks, the Texans were forced to start rookie Dave Ragone against the Jaguars and Bucs during Weeks 14 and 15 of the 2003 season. Ragone couldn't pass for more than 71 yards in either game and didn't account for a single touchdown. The Texans scored a combined three points in those two losses.

Another instance of picking and choosing the right defensive spot is going against a bad backup quarterback. Tony Banks and Chris Chandler can always be counted on to turn the ball over a few times. Look, too, to go against offenses that may have a cluster injury problem in their offensive line or be without their best running back or receiver. Weather can sometimes factor. The Chargers, for instance, shut out the Browns in Cleveland during Week 15 of the 2004 season. The Browns were starting third-string quarterback Luke McCown and the game was played in blowing snow with a subzero wind chill factor. You can sometimes plan for these defensive edges several weeks in advance, giving you ample time to claim a defense in the free agent pool. In 2000, you would have done very well going with whatever defense was playing the Browns that week. Cleveland scored ten or fewer points in eleven of its sixteen games that season and was shut out four times. That happens when Travis Prentice leads your team in rushing and Tim Couch is your quarterback.

Individual Defense Strategy

Some leagues don't use the team defense concept, instead going with individuals. My Rotisserie league uses tackles and sacks as categories. We don't use interceptions because they are too random. If we did, I wouldn't be going after a team's top cornerback, but instead would be looking to draft their number two cornerback. The thinking here is that quarterbacks stay away from testing Champ Bailey, Charles Woodson, and other stud cornerbacks. They go after the weaker corner, meaning that cornerback has more chances to pick off passes. I also would be drafting safeties whose teams use them as centerfielder-types rather than play them up close to help stop the run.

Linebackers

With the exception of the top pass rushers, I like to fill my defensive rosters with linebackers. I'm mainly looking at weakside linebackers, who don't have tight end responsibilities. Linemen don't get many tackles, and not too many defensive tackles get a load of sacks. It's mostly defensive ends who get sacks. Linebackers normally end up with the most tackles and also pick up some sacks. I don't take defensive backs, even though a few safeties like Rodney Harrison annually rack up a lot of tackles. I'm not interested in defensive backs because they rarely get sacks.

Going into 2005, the record for most sacks in a season by a defensive back is seven, set by Dave Duerson of the Bears back in 1986. By comparison, there were thirty-two players in 2004 who recorded more than seven sacks. Only four defensive backs have ever had six or more sacks in a season besides Duerson—Leroy Butler (six in 1996), Harrison (six in 2000), Carnell Lake (six in 1997), and Rod Woodson (six in 1992).

KICKERS

It seemed like a joke at first, and a bad one at that. We were barely into the fourth round of our fantasy football draft and some owner was calling out the name, "Mike Vanderjagt," as in the Colts kicker. He was serious. It was the first time I had ever heard of a kicker going in the first five rounds. You could have a kicker who was Lou "The Toe" Groza, Jan Stenerud, and Tom Dempsey all wrapped into one and he still wouldn't be worth taking that high. No kicker is.

POSITIONS

Kickers are erratic and their statistics differ too much from year to year. With the exception of maybe a half dozen kickers, you never know for sure which kickers are going to score a lot of points. Often they can have a good year percentage-wise, but not put up many points because their offense was bad, or their team happened to score a lot of touchdowns instead of field goals.

A running back can score for you in touchdowns, rushing yards, and receiving yards. Quarterbacks can also score in multiple categories—passing yards, touchdowns and rushing yards. Receivers are good for two categories, receiving yards and touchdowns. They can sometimes get you rushing yards and even passing yards. But kickers score only in kicking points—field goals and extra points. They can't help you in any other category unless they somehow run the ball, catch a pass, or score a touchdown, all of which are highly unlikely.

Just about every league, though, requires at least one kicker in your starting lineup. So you need to familiarize yourself with them. Unlike other positions, talent isn't necessarily the main reason you take a kicker. For example, Jason Hanson might be a top-ten pick instead of usually being an afterthought. Going into the 2005 season, Hanson has made 204 of 213 field goals inside 39 yards. His career accuracy mark is 81 percent, yet less than 9 percent of the owners in ESPN leagues had Hanson on their roster in 2004. The Lions don't have a potent offense, so Hanson gets downgraded.

In studying kickers, you should look at how strong their team's offense is, whether they kick on carpet or grass and if their home games are played in good or bad weather conditions, whether their home stadium is inside a dome, and whether their team has problems scoring touchdowns in the Red Zone. These factors are just as important, if not more important, than talent when judging a kicker. The talent part comes more into play in leagues that award bonus points for long field goals, or leagues that penalize for missed field goals, which places more emphasis on accuracy.

Kickers are the exception to the theory that you can't go wrong grabbing the best player available. The situation is just as important as the skill level. The position is just too dependent on how many field goal attempts a team tries, which is difficult to gauge. For example, let's study the nine-year span from 1996-2004 when there were eight different kickers who led the league in kicking points. The only repeat kicking leader was Jeff Wilkins in 2001 and 2003. Wilkins had everything going for him, kicking for the high-scoring St. Louis Rams, being on carpet in a domed stadium, and playing in an easy division.

In just about every season there were three to four surprise kickers placing in the top ten in points. Kicking leaders range from John Kasay in 1996 to Jay Feely in 2002. The only kickers to consistently place in the top ten during this nine-year stretch were Jason Elam, Adam Vinatieri, Ryan Longwell, Mike Vanderjagt, Jeff Wilkins, David Akers, and Matt Stover. Elam, who has the benefit of kicking for the Broncos in Denver's high altitude, has finished in the top ten seven out of eight years, from 1997-2004. So have Vinatieri and Longwell.

Akers has placed in the top ten each year from 2000-2004. Vanderjagt has been in the top ten five of the six years, from 1999-2004, missing only in 2002. Stover has proven to be an underrated kicker. His name is rarely mentioned among the elite, but he's been in the top ten five of the six years, from 1999-2004, leading the league in 2000. These guys are all solid, reliable kickers, but you never know about the rest. Who would have thought Chargers' rookie Nate Kaeding would finish tenth in kicking points in 2004? On the other hand, one-time dependable Martin Gramatica went so sour he was cut by the Buccaneers during the 2004 season. Just two years earlier, Gramatica had tied for fourth in kicking points after tying for third in 2000. Kickers are a different breed. They can lose their edge sometimes—not physically, but mentally.

Venue is important for a kicker. It's a credit to the Patriots' Vinatieri and the Packers' Longwell that they've annually been among the leaders kicking in bad-weather sites: New England and Green Bay. It's also tough kicking for the Bears, Giants, and Jets because of cold weather and swirling, gusty winds in Chicago and at the Meadowlands. It's difficult kicking in Pittsburgh, too, because of the stadium surface. Kicking in San Francisco isn't much fun either, with wind and unpredictable conditions.

The best places to kick are the domed stadiums. That's always a plus for those kicking in Atlanta, Indianapolis, Minnesota, New Orleans, and St. Louis. Dallas has a partial dome, and Houston has a retractable roof. The weather in Denver can be tricky, but the high altitude is a major plus, as those who have owned Elam can tell you with a grin. Warm weather sites like Arizona, San

Diego, Tampa, and Miami aren't bad either, although it's tough to make a field goal in Miami if you happen to be kicking from the infield dirt.

When to Draft a Kicker

The earliest I ever would take a kicker would be the eleventh round of a draft. Some might go a round or two sooner. Let them. I would be looking at one of the time-tested proven kickers like Akers, Vanderjagt, Elam, Vinatieri, Longwell, Stover, and Wilkins if he has a strong offense behind him. Call them the reliable seven. If these guys are all gone then, my number one factor would be taking a kicker from a powerful offense. This doesn't mean just taking any kicker, though. He has to be decent. Those taking Aaron Elling at the start of 2004 because he was on the high-scoring Vikings got badly burned.

If you miss out on the reliable seven, there's a second tier of good kickers who could contend for the scoring title if their offenses produce. On this list would be the Raiders' Sebastian Janikowski, the Saints' John Carney, the Bengals' Shayne Graham, and the Lions' Jason Hanson. There are only a handful of bad kickers. So there's no reason to panic about landing a kicker. In the last eight years, it has taken an average of 112 points for a kicker to grab a spot among the top ten in kicking points. There were seventeen kickers in 2004 that scored at least 100 points, and eighteen kickers who scored 100 or more points in 2003 and 2002.

Kicking isn't a position where there's a scarcity; there are more than enough kickers to go around. The position is fickle, though. Akers and Vanderjagt certainly seem like the top two heading into 2005, but how many points would they manage if Donovan McNabb and Peyton Manning were to suffer injuries?

Gary Anderson set an NFL record for kicking points in 1998 with 164, making all 35 of his field goal attempts for the Vikings that year. The following season, Anderson finished nineteenth in kicking points, scoring 103. Wilkins is a more recent example of the unpredictable nature of the position. He scored 163 points in 2003, tying the record for most field goals in a season with 39. But in 2004, Wilkins scored just 89 points, finishing behind twenty-three other kickers. So you can see why I'm in no rush to choose my kicker. I'm perfectly content to wait until late in the draft.

FLEX

The most frequently asked question during the fantasy football season is who should be played at flex for the upcoming week. More wrong decisions are made at this spot than any other position. Nearly every fantasy league has a flex, or utility spot, where you can put an extra player in your starting lineup. Usually the position has to be filled by a running back, wide receiver or tight end.

Most weeks it's hard enough coming up with two starting running backs and three wide receivers. So you can understand why it is difficult sometimes to find yet another viable starter. Viable is the key word here. Playing the wrong person at flex can cost you match after match. The player in the flex role should be strong enough to be a legitimate starter, not just someone thrown in to round out your lineup.

You need to take the time and energy to think about this position. It starts at the draft. Think flex. Don't just draft for need. If you've filled out your quarterback, running back, and receiver spots, but there is still a good runner or wideout available, consider taking that player specifically with the flex spot in mind. You don't have to automatically grab your defense, tight end, or kicker once you have your other starters.

Running Back at Flex

Now back to the original question of who to start at flex. It's good to have a running back at flex, but not always possible. Running backs are the rare three-category players who contribute in touchdowns, rushing yards, and receiving yards. Some owners invest their first three draft picks on running backs, thinking that they can start a third one in the flex spot. That makes their team extremely dangerous if they also are able to come up with a good quarterback and enough solid wide receivers. Of course, the third running back has to be good, too.

It's a mistake to throw any running back into the flex position just for the sake of having one there. The object is to score as many points as possible in that spot, not to have a pretty lineup. I have yet to meet anyone who has ever won a fantasy title using his flex spot on Kimble Anders, Larry Centers, Jamel White, or Mike Alstott. These running backs simply don't do enough each week to warrant being fantasy starters.

Some owners won't get their running back until the second or even the third round. That still doesn't rule you out from ever using a runner at flex. Some of the best candidates are the low "B" or high "C" backs usually taken in the middle rounds. Charlie Garner is a good example of this, when he played for the 49ers and Raiders during the 1999 to 2003 seasons. He never scored more than seven touchdowns in a season, so he usually wouldn't be taken until the fourth, fifth, or sixth rounds. Garner wasn't quite strong enough to be your number two runner, but he was perfectly suited to being your flex guy. During those five years he averaged 945 yards rushing and 617 receiving yards.

Quarterback at Flex

Most fantasy owners usually have at least a quarterback, two running backs, and two wide receivers by the end of the sixth round. Those players figure to be their starters. The flex strategy comes in at this point. Here's where you should be looking to see if there still are any NFL starting running backs left, or a highly rated tight end or quality wide receivers.

Barring an injury, it's a safe strategy to play a quarterback at your utility spot if your league rules allow it. You figure to get a couple of touchdowns and 200 passing yards that way, if not any extra rushing yards. Downgrade the quarterback a little, though, if your league takes away points for interceptions and fumbles.

Kickers at Flex

Two of my leagues allow us to use a player from any position at flex. Surprisingly kickers are often put in the flex spot, but I think kickers are your worst choice. Not only do they score in just one category, but their week-to-week success is more random than any other position. You can count on a quarterback and running back to get you at least some points, but you never know what a kicker may give you. His team could score six touchdowns and all he would end up with is six points from six extra point conversions. Meanwhile, your opponent's kicker could exceed that total just by making two field goals and one extra point. Don't waste your precious utility spot on a kicker.

Tight Ends at Flex

Unless by some strange circumstance you had both Tony Gonzalez and Antonio Gates, I would avoid putting a tight end in the flex spot. I used to be hard-line about that philosophy, but I've lessened my stance and am more open-minded to playing an extra tight end following the 2004 season, especially if receptions are factored and not just receiving yards. If you have more than one good tight end, and there's no clear-cut choice to fill your flex spot for the week, consider using your other tight end if going against a defense that has surrendered a lot of yards to tight ends in previous games. Some defenses are geared more to stop wide receivers. They also could have an injury problem at linebacker or safety, which could mean an increased role for the tight end.

Wide Receivers at Flex

Often it comes down to employing one of your extra wide receivers to fill the flex spot. This happens in most leagues where there are more than ten owners because wide receiver is an area that doesn't get watered down with a lot of teams in the league. You should come out of your draft with five or six wide receivers. That provides you with several options during bye weeks. There are also plenty more wide receivers in the free agent pool.

Picking your flex player is easy if you have a really good extra runner or quarterback, rules permitting. More thinking comes into choosing a wide receiver. If you have three or four good ones then it's not a problem, except possibly during bye weeks. Sometimes, however, you have to decide to play it safe or gamble. Possession-type receivers are the more conservative choice. Veterans like Keenan McCardell, Troy Brown, and Marty Booker usually can be counted on to give you some points. Others like Eddie Kennison, Donte Stallworth, and Joey Galloway are more boom-or-bust. They might only get one catch, but it could be for a long touchdown. For instance, Kennison caught three passes for 99 yards and two touchdowns during Week 11 of the 2004 season. The following week he caught just one pass for nine yards. Then in Week 13, he hauled in eight passes for 149 yards and a touchdown.

Some receivers have a history of being inconsistent like Kennison. Sometimes, though, if you manage to come up with a hot receiver at your flex position it pays to stick with him. Derrick Alexander turned out to be a find for fantasy owners in 1996. Following a 1995 season when he caught just 15 passes for 216 yards and no touchdowns for Cleveland, Alexander surfaced with the Ravens the following year. Those owners who took a flyer on him received excellent value when Alexander finished with 1,099 receiving yards and nine touchdowns for Baltimore in '96.

Matchups

Matchups are an important tool when deciding who to start at flex. Your choice probably comes down to four or five players. See which ones are playing at home that week, which ones are going up against bad defenses, and which might be involved in a game where weather could impact their statistics.

Let's use Week 15 of the 2003 season as an illustration. Hypothetically, let's assume you have solid starters, but have yet to settle on who to use at flex. Your choices come down to running back Amos Zereoue and wide receivers Rod Gardner, Corey Bradford, Tai Streets, and Brandon Stokley. There's no surefire starter there, so you need to break down each player's matchup for the week.

Your first inclination is to go with the running back. Zereoue, who was the Steelers' second-string running back that season, is a scatback type who gets spot carries and passes thrown to him out of the backfield. He can break big plays, but is not going to get a lot of carries. This is a mid-December game against the Jets on the road, so you need to check the weather. Sure enough, there's snow and sleet. That's not conducive to Zereoue's speedy style at all. So cross him off. Result: Jets beat the Steelers, 6-0, and Zereoue rushes seven times for 24 yards.

Gardner would be a safe choice. He's a solid receiver for Washington. However, the Redskins are on the road at Dallas and backup Tim Hasselbeck is Washington's starting quarterback for the game. Cross off Gardner. Result: Cowboys win 27-0 and Gardner is held to three receptions for 24 yards.

Bradford would be the riskiest pick. He's a dangerous, deep threat for Houston, averaging nearly 20 yards a catch. But the Texans are away from home against the Bucs, who have the third-best pass defense in the NFL. I'd say the odds aren't good of Bradford burning them. Cross off Bradford.

Streets, on the other hand, is a dependable number two possession receiver for the 49ers going against the Bengals, who rank twenty-second in pass defense. The game is on the road. The 49ers haven't won a road game. Still, there should be enough leftovers from Terrell Owens for Streets to put up a respectable number. Put Streets under consideration. Result: Bengals win 41-38 and Streets catches six balls for 89 yards and scores a touchdown.

The last choice is Stokley, who is with the Colts and has Peyton Manning as his quarterback. Stokley fits into the category of going with a player from a powerful offense for your flex spot. The thinking here is that a great offense puts up enough yards to go around for everyone. But Stokley hasn't caught a touchdown pass so far. Should he be eliminated from the decision-making process because of that? Maybe he's due. This could be his breakout game considering the Falcons have one of the all-time worst defenses and rank last in pass defense. The Colts are also at home, and the Falcons fired Dan Reeves during the week, so their preparation and focus may be off. Stokley's our man. Result: Colts win 38-7 and

Stokley catches seven passes for 95 yards and scores two touchdowns.

Flex Summary

This is the kind of analysis you need to do when deciding on your flex player. Yes, it takes some time, and you're still not going to be right all the time. Some of your decisions may backfire no matter how much sense the reasoning may make. But more times than not, by studying the situation a little closer, you'll make the right call. Make enough right calls and you'll be on your way to winning your league.

9. POST DRAFT

PICKUPS

If you think you can relax once your draft is finished, think again. Now the real work begins. Sorry, but you need to keep staying on top of things. You can win a league having a great draft and getting lucky avoiding injuries. You can also win a league by making astute free agent pickups once the season begins. An owner who placed first in a high-end 2004 league said one of the biggest factors in his winning the championship was picking up Muhsin Muhammad from the free agent pool.

Some leagues allow you to replace an injured player right after your draft. Resist that temptation. If your league allows it, make your replacement choice after opening week unless you have to fill a starting spot. All thirty-two teams are in action Week 1. So you'll have plenty of free agent choices. There are going to be the usual surprises, injuries, and hidden gems emerging after opening week. Think back to Week 1 of the 2003 season. Anquan Boldin set a rookie record in the Cardinals' opener against the Lions. Boldin caught 10 passes for 217 yards and scored two touchdowns. That was a 43-point fantasy performance in leagues that count six points for touchdowns, one point for every 10 yards receiving, and one point per reception.

Boldin had been available in virtually every free pool, but no longer was after that game. It wasn't a fluke. Boldin finished his rookie season with 101 catches for 1,377 yards and eight touchdowns. Ironically, Boldin was one of the injured players you could have taken at the 2004 draft. One owner did, choosing Boldin in the third round. After the draft someone asked him why he took Boldin so high.

"Because he had such a great year last year," the Boldin owner replied.

"Yeah, but he's hurt," said another owner.

"You're kidding," said the Boldin owner. "I didn't know that. When did he get hurt?"

How come there are never any owners like that in my leagues?

In sharper leagues, there are slim pickings in the free agent pool toward the end of the season. But in the beginning, there are plenty to choose from in case one of your players gets hurt, or you want to get rid of a player who isn't doing well for you. If a player does emerge, and is in the free agent pool, chances are there will be multiple claims on him. Most leagues operate where the team lowest in the standings gets him. So you need to be able to project a week or two in advance in order to land a potential prize. This is even more crucial if your league uses a first-come, first-serve basis for picking up players.

However, don't go overboard on a journeyman player who might have happened to have a nice game the week before. Ricky Proehl-types are always going to be number four receivers. Study the circumstances. Perhaps a wide receiver had a big game because of an injury, was going against a weak secondary, or matched up against a "dime" back while the better cornerbacks were guarding the other receivers.

Keep an eye on backup running backs, recognize who the good number three wideouts are, and be aware of where there could be possible quarterback changes. If you have the roster size, try throwing a few darts on backup runners, especially on teams with unsettled running back situations. When Michael Bennett wasn't able to play during the first half of the 2004 season, astute owners grabbed Onterrio Smith. But once Smith was taken, Mewelde Moore should have emerged on your radar screen, especially with veteran Moe Williams also being hurt. Sure enough, Smith got suspended and Moore took over as the starter, putting up several huge all-purpose yardage games before getting injured himself.

Look at Quarterbacks

It is rare to land a quality starting quarterback in free agency. But quarterback injuries and starting switches happen frequently. Some quarterbacks never seem to get hurt, so don't waste a roster spot holding on to the backups for Brett Favre, Peyton Manning, Tom Brady, and Daunte Culpepper. The backup has to be decent. It certainly wasn't worth owning Rodney Peete, Ken Dorsey, Jonathan Quinn, and Phillip Rivers in 2004. These guys weren't capable of producing consistent starter's numbers.

The time to act on a backup quarterback in free agency is when you notice the first-stringer continually not playing well or battling injuries. That's the time to stash that team's backup on your roster, if you have the space. Steve McNair took a heavy battering during the first half of 2004, and was eventually forced to sit out the final five games. His backup, Billy Volek, helped some fantasy owners win their leagues by throwing for a combined 918 yards and eight touchdowns during Weeks 14 and 15.

Volek made an excellent pickup because he has skills and the Titans were forced to pass a lot because of multiple injuries that rendered their defense totally ineffective. Don't waste a free agent move, though, on quality backups if they have no chance of playing even if the starting quarterback isn't playing well. This entails knowing the team's situation and attitude of the coach.

Carson Palmer is an example from 2004. No matter how many mistakes the second-year Palmer made, he wasn't going to be pulled for veteran Jon Kitna unless he got hurt. Bengals management made it clear that Palmer was the future of the franchise and they were sticking with him. It was the same with the Ravens and their young quarterback, Kyle Boller.

Look at Match-ups

Keep in mind bye weeks when making free agent pickups. Try to plan a week or two in advance of them. If it's Week 2 and your defense has a bye on Week 5, it's not too early to dip into the free agent pool and project which available defense will be best during Week 5. Study the matchups for that upcoming week. See who the home teams are. It's the same with position players. Are there guys in the free agent pool that could be really good during a certain week because of the defense they're going against?

I won the championship game in my online league in 1999 by taking wide receivers Tim Dwight of the Falcons and J.J. Stokes of the 49ers in the free agent pool a week before Atlanta played its final game of the season against the 49ers in a meaningless Monday night game. I figured the teams would be loose and there would be a lot of scoring.

So I started Dwight and Stokes along with Jeff Garcia, the 49ers quarterback, knowing the Falcons had the sixth-worst defense. The 49ers won 34-29. Garcia threw for 373 yards and accounted for three touchdowns. Dwight caught seven passes for 162 yards and had three touchdowns. Even Stokes chipped in with five receptions for 130 yards and a touchdown. My opponent was beating me going into that final game. But with those performances I easily won the match and title.

If you're going to get caught short at wide receiver or another position during a bye week, head the problem off before it happens. Don't do it too early, because the NFL landscape changes so much, but do it at least a week or two ahead of time if you have the roster maneuverability. That way you can scheme matchups, taking a player in a favorable expectation spot. This is better than just grabbing a body at the last moment, hoping for a miracle performance. Try to separate one-week wonders from legitimate prospects.

There were reasons why Dwight and Stokes were in the free agent pool. They made for a great spot play against the Falcons that final game of the '99 season, but keep things in perspective. Don't get caught up thinking that because a free agent pickup has a great game for you, he's going to do it every week.

Try not to make the same mistake I did in Week 8 of the 2004 season when I needed a running back for that Sunday. My choice came down to the Titans' Antowain Smith or New England's Kevin Faulk, both backups. The team's starters, Chris Brown and Corey Dillon, were both questionable that week. I went for Smith because the Titans were playing the Bengals, who ranked last in rush defense, and I considered Brown more fragile than Dillon.

Jeff Fisher and Bill Belichick didn't make my decision easy. These two coaches never revealed their starting running back until game time. By then it was too late, since I had to make my move on Friday afternoon. Brown played the entire game, rushing for 147 yards and scoring a touchdown. Smith didn't get a single carry. Making it sting even worse was that my opponent that week in my head-to-head league had Brown.

Belichick, the ultimate sandbagger, didn't play Dillon that week. Faulk didn't have nearly the game Brown did, but in hindsight I should have gone with Faulk, or at least hedged since I took Smith in another league where I had an opening. The Titans were off the following week, while the Patriots played against the soft Rams run defense. So I ended up getting a fat zero and letting Smith go the following week. I should have done a better job in my decision-making of taking the Titans' Week 9 bye into account. Naturally Smith ended up filling in for Brown a couple of weeks later. By that time, though, I couldn't get Smith.

Other Considerations

A lot, too, depends on your league format. The leagues I participate in limit you to two free agent moves a week and one waiver pickup. A player on waivers is someone who was cut from another owner's roster the week before. He is therefore on waivers the following week, eligible to be picked up. If no one claims him during that one week he goes into the general free agent pool. You don't want to be making moves just to shuffle bodies around, especially if there are transaction fees involved and you're in a league that plays with a salary cap where you have a set limit to purchase free agents. The pickup has to make sense. If the player you're trying to obtain isn't any better than the player you're cutting, it's not worth it. If there is no upside, what's the point?

DROPS

Picking up a new player is easy. The hard part is releasing a player to make room. *Be patient*, I tell myself every year. Yet I still end up dropping somebody too soon. In 2004, I did it with 49ers linebacker Jamie Winborn in a league that counts tackles and sacks. Fed up with Winborn's slow start, I dropped him before the start of Week 6. Of course he went on to get eleven solo tackles that Sunday, and followed it up with five solo tackles and two sacks his next game.

Here's where temperament factors in when deciding whether or not to keep a player. Don't ever get too high or down on a player based on just one performance. Chances are he's not as good or bad as he looked in one game. There could be extenuating circumstances that affected his showing, like a hidden injury, specific game plan, or a blocking scheme.

A proven quality player eventually emerges. Sometimes it just takes the right situation. On the other hand, you can't wait forever or be that patient. Your fantasy football season can be as short as thirteen weeks, depending on your playoff structure. So if a player, no matter how good he has been in the past, isn't getting the ball enough, you have to make a move, even if it pains you. It became clear when Eli Manning replaced Kurt Warner as the Giants' starting quarterback ten games into the 2004 season that Amani Toomer wasn't going to finish with his typical season. Toomer had gone above 1,000 receiving yards each of the previous six years, while scoring 31 touchdowns during that time period. But Toomer ended up with 747 yards receiving and failed to score a single touchdown in 2004.

Before you drop a decent player, at least try to trade him, even if it means getting very little in return. Don't waste people's time, though, if the player is a stiff. Remember I said *decent player*. I was offered Travis Henry, for example, in exchange for kicker Phil Dawson. The Henry owner wanted a kicker, and realized Henry held little value anymore. I liked Henry, but it was clear he had lost his starting spot to Willis McGahee and wasn't going to get many carries. So I shopped Dawson around to owners who might be interested in another kicker. This was in a league that required two kickers. At the time Dawson was at peak value, having the third most kicking points and the NFL's longest consecutive field goal streak. I ended up trading Dawson and Jake Plummer for Fred Taylor.

Bye Weeks

Drops are very important when preparing for bye weeks. You need to have a competitive lineup going for you every week. This isn't fantasy baseball with its 162-game schedule, where you can let an injured guy sit and not replace him if he's out just a short while. You need to be well acquainted with the free agent pool, which means dropping a player to pick up a player. The hard part sometimes isn't figuring out which free agent to get, but who to drop in order to get that player. Some candidates might be a second tight end, an underachieving wide receiver, or a backup running back that even if he did play, it would just be in a platoon role. That was the case with Musa Smith, who some thought of as the main backup to Jamal Lewis. But when Lewis sat out two games in 2004 because of suspension and missed a couple of others because of an ankle injury, it was Chester Taylor and not Smith who got most of the touches.

Running backs, though, have the highest standard. It's hard to find as many quality running backs in the free pool as any of the other positions. Owners tend to cling to their backup runners. Sometimes holding on to one can pay off in a big way as it did in 2001 when Colts' backup Dominic Rhodes replaced an injured Edgerrin James in Game 7 and finished the season with 1,104 yards and nine touchdowns. Many times, though, you're just wasting a bench spot. Case in point is LaMont Jordan in 2002, 2003, and 2004. Jordan never gained more than 480 yards in any of those three seasons, despite being considered one of the better backups, because he was stuck behind the durable Curtis Martin.

The Seahawks' Maurice Morris is another example. Some owner always scooped Morris up at the end of the draft, hoping the Seattle reserve running back would get a chance if Shaun Alexander ever got hurt. Well guess what? Going into 2005, it has never worked. Morris has had 100 carries in his three years with the Seahawks since coming into the league in 2002. The most carries Morris has had in a season is 38. Alexander carried the ball 974 times during this three-year span of 2002-2004.

There's no reason to carry more than one tight end, unless you have two of the top seven. If so, you need to trade one. There's always a Freddie Jones-quality free agent floating around in the tight end pool when your regular one has his bye week. Extra wide receivers are good candidates to be dropped. Getting one back isn't a problem. The free agent pool is full of them. There are usually wide receivers to be found who make good start-ers in certain weeks, or who get better as the season pro-gresses like Nate Burleson did for the Vikings and rookie Lee Evans did for the Bills in 2004.

POST DRAFT

Patience

Study the makeup of the free agent pool and upcoming schedule before making your drops. If you're ready to drop a starter who has been disappointing, but whose next few games are against weak defenses, then maybe hold on to him an extra week or two. If there's a scarcity of starting quarterbacks in the free pool, then perhaps think twice about releasing one of your quarterbacks. Be in the middle with your attitude—be patient when a player isn't doing as well as expected, but don't be so stubborn or egotistical that you won't make a move. That sometimes means admitting a mistake.

Sometimes you make the hard decision to finally drop a borderline talent, and the player immediately starts producing. Yeah, it bites. But that kind of thing happens all the time. Play fantasy football long enough and it will happen to you, too. If it does, don't dwell on it. One owner was beating himself up for cutting Brandon Stokley two games into the 2004 season. Stokley went on to finish with 1,077 receiving yards and 10 touchdowns. But Stokley only had 104 receiving yards going into Week 3.

He had never caught more than 24 passes in his five previous years in the NFL, and was the Colts' number three receiver behind Marvin Harrison and Reggie Wayne. As it turned out, the Colts became the first team ever to have three receivers finish with more than 1,000 reception yards and at least 10 touchdowns apiece. The Stokley owner is being way too hard on himself. It's easy to second-guess after the season. What you have to take into consideration is when you made the move. Was the timing right at the time?

10. TRANSACTIONS

Rarely, if ever, can you win a league championship by relying solely on the players you drafted—not with injuries occurring so frequently and the way things change so rapidly in the NFL. You must always keep looking for ways to improve your team. It means picking up and discarding players. These methods are done through the waiver wire, free agent pool, and making trades.

Sometimes it becomes clear very early in the season that you made a drafting mistake. To rectify that, there is the waiver wire and free agent pool. Other times you think a trade can improve your team, so you'll try to make a deal. Let's look at these options by starting with the waiver wire.

Waiver Wire

When an owner cuts a player to pick up somebody else, the released player goes on **waivers**. This means that the player is then eligible to be picked up by any team, going into effect the following week. Usually the last place team has first choice, followed by second-to-last and so on up. In most leagues the team that cut the player has the last waiver claim.

If no one claims the player during the week, he goes into the general **free agent pool** the following week. It takes at least a week into the season before the waiver wire gets active. Once injuries and more attractive players emerge, owners start making moves.

Free Agent Pool

The **free agent pool** is the most popular way to get a new player. The free agent pool consists of every player who wasn't drafted in your league. Don't expect to find any superstars there, but usually there are some promising players, especially early in the season. Every year there seems to be hidden sleepers in the free agent pool, who because of injuries or nonproduction from the starter get the opportunity to become useful fantasy performers.

Some even turn out to be fantasy monsters. Some free agent stars from 2004 who weren't originally drafted in most leagues include Reuben Droughns, Nick Goings, Michael Clayton, Jason Witten, Eric Johnson, Ronald Curry, Larry Johnson, Eddie Kennison, Drew Brees, Brandon Stokley, Nate Burleson, Ben Roethlisberger, Brian Griese, Billy Volek, and T. J. Houshmandzadeh.

The free agent pool can be used for many reasons. There are injuries, of course. You can dip into the pool to strengthen your reserves, or pick up a quality backup. The well is full of players in case you want to pick somebody up because one of your players isn't doing the job. You might spot somebody in there you could use for trade bait, such as an extra quarterback. Often, too, there are impact players such as the above mentioned, who for some reason or another were overlooked at the draft.

Roster Moves

Keep in mind, though, picking up a free agent involves cutting one of your players. Some leagues allow you to reserve your injured players, picking a free agent to replace him. The two players then become an entry, tied together. So when your injured player becomes healthy, you have to either keep him or his replacement. Sometimes it can be a tough choice. If you like the replacement player and don't want to lose him, you can slide him into an open spot if you happen to have another player listed as out. You must have an opening, though. Usually you have two weeks to make a move or you automatically lose the player.

This can also lead to a favorable trading situation if the player you temporarily picked up turns out well. You can offer him and another player to an owner for a good player and a stiff in a two-for-two deal. The stiff would be for the replacement, so he becomes tied to the injured player. Since your injured player is now healthy and waiting to be activated, you just cut the stiff and activate your now healthy player. Meanwhile, you've gotten an edge on the second part of the deal by getting a good player. The other owner might be willing to do it if he's desperate to get rid of a stiff and doesn't see anybody he's particularly attracted to in the free agent pool.

Transactions Costs

There's a **transaction cost** in many leagues for making moves. In our face-to-face league, for example, each transaction costs $5. It's the same cost for a waiver move and trade. Using my face-to-face league as an example again, it would cost you $5 to reserve an injured player, $5 to pick up his replacement, and then another $5 to activate the injured player when he's ready to come back. So if budget is a consideration, you need to be judicious making free agent moves. You don't want to spend more than you can afford or have budgeted.

A lot of leagues restrict how many transactions you can make in a week, or give you a yearly salary budget that you can't exceed. This, and having to cut one of your players, keeps owners from dipping into the free pool too heavily.

Making Moves to Win

Making moves is essential to be a winner at fantasy football. But sometimes patience is needed. If a proven player has a bad first couple of weeks, don't give up on him too fast. Defenses and game plans have a lot to do with performance. All NFL players possess a certain talent level. A lot has to do with opportunity and getting touches. Give even the most mediocre running back 30 carries against a bad defense and he's going to put up numbers. The Panthers' Nick Goings is proof of that. He put up five 100-yard rushing games during the second half of the 2004 season after Stephen Davis, DeShaun Foster, Brad Hoover, Rod Smart, and Joey Harris all suffered injuries.

The first thing I look for each week in fantasy football is my league standings. The next thing I look at is the free agent pool and waiver wire. It's that important. It's the life support system to your team.

BLOCKING

Blocking basically involves grabbing a free agent you don't really need in order to keep that player away from another owner. This move isn't necessarily about upgrading your bench. It's a defensive maneuver targeting a position area or specific player on waivers or free agency. Your purpose is to prevent that player from going to an owner who might have a desperate need at that position.

We're not talking offensive linemen here. This isn't about guards or tackles, but a sophisticated move designed to prevent your opponent, or nearest competitor, from helping himself in the free agent pool.

Quarterbacks and kickers are the best examples. Let's say you're in a fourteen-owner league. Each owner has two quarterbacks. A couple of owners even have three. That leaves just two starting quarterbacks in the free agent pool. Your opponent that week may have one injured quarterback and another on a bye. He has to find a replacement quarterback for this particular week.

Realizing that, you go into the free agent pool, and put in for the best remaining starting quarterback. If you're lower in the standing, or have a higher bid in leagues using that type of format, you snatch the quarterback away from your needier opponent. It doesn't matter if you have two stronger quarterbacks already on your roster. The move is intended to hurt your opponent, not strengthen your roster. You'll probably look to even cut that quarterback the following week when you face a new opponent.

Kickers are another common blocking example. Some owners make it a priority to draft a backup kicker just so they don't get caught short on a bye week or if an injury occurs. Kickers don't usually get hurt, but you never know. Four starting kickers missed at least two games during the 2004 season because of injury, and several others were questionable at various parts of the season. Because of a bye, your opponent may need a kicker for the week. Let's say there are six left in the free agent pool. Other owners might be looking for a kicker, too, if their main kicker is on a bye. Of the remaining free agent kickers, one is kicking in a dome that week against a bad defense. The others are on the road and either aren't very consistent, or don't kick for high-scoring teams. You have one of the best kickers in the league. He's your starter this week, but you might consider blocking your opponent by putting in a claim or bid for the best remaining free agent kicker. Kickers are certainly not as important as the skill position players, but nobody likes to go into a matchup without one. Blocking can do that to your opponent.

Here's a running back blocking illustration from the 2004 season. Tennessee tailback Chris Brown is questionable with a turf toe injury. His backup is Antowain Smith, who is in the free agent pool. You're playing against the team whose owner has Brown. That owner needs another running back.

Obviously he is going to be interested in Smith. You realize that. You check out his remaining free agent budget and find out you have enough to outbid him. So you do it. You end up with Smith. The other owner comes up empty-handed or with a lesser running back. Your chances of winning the matchup have increased. Congratulations, that's a smart block.

Blocking may seem mean-spirited to some, but it's not dirty pool. You're following the rules. It's strategy. There's enough luck in fantasy football, so if you can do anything legal to improve your chances of winning, then do it. It's up to each owner to plan ahead for bye weeks and have good roster management and enough of a budget left to pick up a key free agent when needed. A top owner not only knows his roster, but is aware of his opponent's roster, too.

What's not kosher is asking another owner in your league to pick up a player in order to better your chances. Each owner has to do what's best for his team, not someone else's squad. If the last-place owner is clueless, it's not your job to point out to him potential gems in the free agent pool. It's not fair to other owners hoping to get certain players.

A negative to blocking can be hurt feelings. Some owners may feel it's a cheap stunt and take it personally if you keep them from taking a player they urgently want when you really don't have use for the player. They consider that unsportsmanlike. Hopefully owners realize it's not a personal thing, but sound strategy on your part. Human nature being as it is, though, there's the possibility, especially in nonsophisticated leagues, that they will consider it plain malicious on your part to block.

Owners who feel this way may not trade with you. It's not worth making an enemy. So consider your league makeup when deciding whether blocking is warranted or not. If you're in a small stakes, buddies-type league, perhaps it doesn't pay to block, or at least make multiple blocks on a position your opponent is caught short in. But in other leagues, especially high-end money leagues, the level is raised. There's probably going to be more tolerance and understanding of this maneuver.

MAKING TRADES

You want a third running back and are willing to pay a fair price to get one. So you offer a solid "B" wide receiver, say Joe Horn, for a low "B" running back like Warrick Dunn. It's a no-brainer, right? It's fair for both teams, correct? Even so, your trade offer gets rejected. The problem wasn't your offer, but what your opponent needed.

If the team you want to trade with is already loaded at wide receiver, he probably doesn't care to take another wideout no matter how good the offer. Studying your opponent's needs is as essential as trying to improve your own team when attempting to make a deal.

It's easy to know what you need. The tricky part is finding a way to solve that need. As mentioned earlier, you have three options when trying to get a new player— free agency, waivers, or making a trade. Pulling off a trade is the hardest. Once you target the position you need the most help in, check out who is available in the free agent pool. Maybe you can also find a replacement on the waiver wire. These avenues are less risky because you have the choice of who to cut to pick up this player.

You can get a much better player through trading, but you're going to give up a decent player in return. That's fine if you have excess at a certain position, or are running away with a category and want to achieve better balance. Just remember it takes two to trade. Elite quarterbacks and running backs are the hardest to obtain. Do you have the goods to get one? Don't waste someone's time offering a fourth-round choice for a player taken in the top twelve. Even if the person you want to get a wide receiver from is running away with the category, he's not going to trade you Randy Moss for Duce Staley.

You'd be correct, though, to target the team that is leading in the category in which you want to improve. I don't make too many trade offers. But the ones I make are treated very seriously because I've done my homework. In a meticulously written e-mail to the owner I want to trade with, I explain why this trade offer helps him. You can only do this by carefully studying his roster. You can do some spinning in your negotiations, but never lie.

For instance, I traded Akili Smith during the 2000 season and received a top defensive player in return. (Tackles and sacks are categories in this particular league.) Smith started eleven games for the Bengals that season. He threw three touchdown passes and completed less than 45 percent of his passes.

In my trade negotiations I never dwelled on the fact that Smith very well could be a bust, but pointed out how Cincinnati had taken him with the number three overall pick and how Smith had shown so much potential in college. Smith could settle down now that the starting job was his. Two years later Smith was out of the NFL.

At the time, the trade didn't seem that lopsided since Smith had just been named the Bengals' starting quarterback. What I can't stand are stupid trade offers that are absolute rip-offs and make no sense. Curious as to what one owner was thinking when he made a particularly odious offer, I e-mailed back, rejecting the trade and asking, "Why would I make this deal?" The message back was, "I didn't make the offer to help you." Sometimes if I receive a bad trade offer, I'll write back asking if the owner were in my shoes would he make that trade? The usual response is, "Well no, but ..."

Look, if you're going to make a trade offer, do it right. Take the time to analyze not only your own needs, but what it would take for your opponent to deal the player or players you want. If your opponent has a running back you crave and is last in kicking points, don't just offer him a kicker. A kicker doesn't equal a good running back. Make a two-for-one offer of your best kicker and a lesser runner or starting wide receiver for a decent running back.

If you're targeting a superstar, step up to the plate. If you want Shaun Alexander and the owner who has him needs a quarterback, then offer Donovan McNabb. At the very least offer him a "B" quarterback such as Brett Favre or Trent Green and see where the negotiations go.

I'll tell you what's frustrating. You want a certain player, so you spend the time coming up with a fair offer that definitely helps both teams and then that other owner rejects it because he either wants to rip you off, or is too conservative to trade. We have one such owner in my league. He rarely finishes in the money, yet won't trade.

Needing a quarterback in a league where you can start up to three of them, I turned to this owner since he was the only owner with four starting quarterbacks. He had Peyton Manning and was running away with the passing category. However, he was last in receiving. I offered him Randy Moss for Manning. Rejected. Okay, I then offered him any of my other starting wide receivers, all of whom were decent and better than his heap of low "C" wideouts. Nope. It got to the point where I was so worn out and desperate for a quarterback that week I offered Jerry Porter for Jay Fielder. Nope.

Exasperated, I asked this owner why he never dealt. His reply was, "When people come to me to trade, they're trying to rip me off. Why else would they want to trade? They don't care about my best interests." This owner is hopeless. He actually is a brilliant person with a high IQ, Ivy League education, and a successful professional football handicapper, but he'll never succeed in fantasy football until he changes his rigid behavior. Trading is one of the outlets you have to improve your team. Why close it off?

But if someone absolutely won't trade, don't waste your energy on him. In assessing your opponent's needs, you must take into account his willingness to deal. There are owners who are the exact opposite of the one I just discussed. They love to trade. Bye weeks can be the most opportune time to deal, because owners get shorthanded then. Sometimes they'll panic and end up making a bad deal just to have a full roster that week. So not only target players you want, but take into consideration the other owner and timing of the deal. Maybe that owner would be more willing to deal in two weeks when both his starting running backs are on byes.

Try to find out if an owner has biases. Some owners want to collect as many players from their favorite team as possible. We had an owner like that. Unfortunately for him, his favorite team was the Bears. His list of quarterbacks through the years read like a Stephen King novel. You knew he was in trouble when he showed up at the draft one year wearing a Cade McNown jersey. Then he compounded his fashion gaffe by actually drafting Mc-Nown.

Another owner took great pride owning Emmitt Smith one year. Emmitt was his longtime favorite player. Funny, but that owner didn't have a whole lot of competition anymore getting Smith after Smith joined the Arizona Cardinals. Sometimes you can't help but get attached to certain players. But don't let any misguided loyalty delude you into making stupid decisions. If someone should offer you a better player for your favorite player, well, say good-bye to your favorite player.

PROTESTING TRADES

Wouldn't it be great if every trade was balanced and fair? Sometimes it happens. Other times, though, you see a deal so lopsided you're left wondering if you should actually protest. In many online leagues such as Yahoo and ESPN, there is a **protest function**.

With this function, trades are posted and owners have several days to register a protest simply by checking the protest box. It's good to have this protective device, especially when money is involved. The nastiest word in fantasy sports is collusion. That's when two or more competing owners make a deal to help one win, with both splitting the profits.

High-end money leagues often don't permit trading. They don't want to take chances on any possibility of collusion. Luckily, collusion is almost never a problem because people play fantasy sports because they love the thrill of honest competition and the chance to put their opinions into play. The thought of collusion would never enter their brain for a second. Still, it doesn't hurt to have a safeguard in place.

Only once in more than fifteen years of doing multiple fantasy football, baseball, and basketball leagues have I encountered collusion. It was in a face-to-face keeper baseball league where two friends made a six-for-six deal where one owner got all the other guy's superstars and didn't give him any good potential keepers back to balance the deal. It was stars for stiffs. The stench was obvious.

Our commissioner immediately stepped in and voided the deal, asking the rest of the league if these two morally bankrupt owners should be permanently removed from the league. The answer was a unanimous yes. It turned out that one of the owners nursed a lingering grudge against the league because he rarely finished in the money and had a hard time making deals. It never occurred to him to make better trade offers. His partner was more passive, having to be talked into the scheme. But he had participated, so he had to go, too.

TRANSACTIONS

The commissioner did the right thing. If it doesn't have integrity, your league is no good. A hard line has to be taken. Hopefully, you'll never encounter such a situation. It's doubtful you will.

Now back to protesting trades. I never protest a trade unless I suspect collusion or the trade is just too ridiculous. These values have been severely tested. One of the worst trades I encountered was in a 2001 online league when an owner dealt Marvin Harrison, a top-three wide receiver, for Antowain Smith, a "C" running back. Clearly, that wasn't a fair deal.

Even though it was a huge rip-off, I didn't protest. The owner dealing Harrison had an abundance of wide receivers and desperately wanted a starting running back. This owner wasn't a moron as you might have thought. He was a college football beat writer for a major daily newspaper. Of course, that doesn't qualify him for brain surgery, but he did know the players. He just panicked and made a horrendous deal. Maybe he felt Smith was suddenly going to become Jim Brown reincarnated. Whatever the case, I didn't think it fair to protest a deal between the two owners.

I don't like it when someone protests one of my deals, so I rarely protest someone else's trade. It's important to stay on the welcome mat with your fellow league owners. One way to alienate at least two of them is to protest a deal, especially if it's a legitimate deal or even semi-legitimate. Always keep in mind the subjective factor. Owners see players differently. Not everybody has the same opinions. Also, there could be hidden reasons why an owner made a deal, such as trying to upgrade a certain weakness, being too strong or weak at a position, obtaining his favorite player from his favorite team, or even trading for a player with another trade in mind. You just don't know. If you see a trade that you don't think is fair, at least try to keep an open mind. Also keep friendly with the owner you believe got the short end of the stick. You never know. Maybe he'll make a deal with you!

If you honestly believe a trade is too lopsided and would hurt the league, then go ahead and protest. But e-mail the league, or post a message on the Web site bulletin board, explaining your reasons for protesting. Don't do it anonymously, either. Be as polite as possible and hopefully everyone will understand you had the good of the league at heart.

11. TRENDS

Being one of the first to pick up on a trend can lead to winning your fantasy league title. Trends can be spotted easily enough, but adjusting to them rapidly can be difficult. Flexibility is once again key.

The NFL did some tinkering with its illegal contact rule prior to the 2004 season. The league made it clear that after the Patriots' defensive backs mugged the Colts wide receivers during the 2003 AFC championship game that officials would put more emphasis on enforcing the chuck rule, where a defender can't touch a receiver after five yards.

This did indeed open up the passing game, while making quarterbacks and tight ends more valuable in fantasy football. Going into the 2004 season, star running backs were by far the most desirable fantasy players. Nearly every fantasy football publication advised taking runners.

Halfway through the season, though, it was clear that quarterbacks were the dominant fantasy scorers. Through the first ten weeks, the top fantasy point-getters were quarterbacks Peyton Manning, Daunte Culpepper, Donovan McNabb, Drew Brees, Jake Plummer, and Brett

Favre. By the end of the year, nine quarterbacks ranked among the top sixteen fantasy producers. The biggest beneficiaries weren't so much wide receivers but tight ends. Some of them broke team records for most receptions in a season by a tight end.

Those fantasy owners that speedily reacted to this by picking up free agents such as Antonio Gates, Jason Witten, and Eric Johnson, while trading a runner for a top quarterback, were amply rewarded. Trends aren't always this obvious. Some are more subtle, but each season yields something worth reviewing. The astute owners pick up these things and aren't afraid to change on the fly. Often that's what separates them from the rest of the pack. It's important to have some idea of recent history to learn lessons and avoid repeating mistakes. So let's go back to the past six years and see what trends and developments happened during this time in fantasy football:

YEAR 1999

This was one of the worst years ever for injuries, as eight of the top fifteen fantasy producers in 1998 missed significant portions of the '99 season, including Terrell Davis, Steve Young, Jamal Anderson, and Garrison Hearst. This had a trickle down effect on team and individual performances. Terrell Owens, for instance, had 1,097 receiving yards and 14 touchdowns in 1998 with Young throwing to him that season. But with Young playing only three games in 1999, Owens's production dwindled to 754 receiving yards and four touchdowns.

The "you can't be a fantasy stud forever" realization hit home during this season. Both Dan Marino and Jerry Rice slipped noticeably. This ended up being Marino's final year. He passed for 2,448 yards and 12 touchdowns. He still had been effective in 1998, throwing for 3,497 yards and tossing 23 touchdowns. Rice had his fewest receiving yards since coming into the NFL in 1985, not including 1997 when he was limited to just two games because of an injury. Rice had 327 fewer receiving yards than he had had in '98. He scored just five touchdowns after reaching the end zone nine times in '98. This showed that even the best at their position reach a slowing down period.

YEAR 2000

In this season we learned you can gain a decided edge if you absolutely blow away the competition at a minor spot like defense and tight end. The Ravens rode a dominant defense to a Super Bowl title, holding foes under 251 yards ten times and under 11 points eleven times, while shutting out four teams. No other fantasy defense came close to those numbers.

Tony Gonzalez scored nearly 70 fantasy points more than the next closest tight end in 2000 with 93 receptions for 1,203 yards and nine touchdowns. Those fantasy owners lucky enough to have the Ravens defense and Gonzalez didn't need a franchise running back or stud quarterback to win a title, showing it can be done without those major ingredients.

YEAR 2001

This season reinforced the belief that rookie running backs can succeed as LaDainian Tomlinson, Anthony Thomas, and Dominic Rhodes all produced big seasons. In turn, this season reinforced the notion that rookie wide receivers rarely make much of an impact. Chris Chambers and Rod Gardner were the only rookie wideouts to rank among the sixty wide receivers.

This turned out to be a strong year for quarterbacks, but there was a trend showing quarterbacks switching teams struggled their first season with a new club. Elvis Grbac ranked sixth in fantasy production for quarterbacks in 2000 when he played with the Chiefs. But his passing yards were down 1,131 yards with the Ravens in 2001. His completion percentage went from 59 percent to 56 percent and he threw four more interceptions. Trent Green had a difficult time operating the Chiefs offense for the first time after coming from the Rams. Matt Hasselbeck struggled as a first-year starter for the Seahawks after being a backup in Green Bay.

YEAR 2002

We had a changing of the guard at wide receiver during this season. Fantasy owners needed to realize that veterans Tim Brown, Troy Brown, Ed McCaffrey, David Boston, Johnnie Morton, and Qadry Ismail were descending, while a number of younger wide receivers were emerging such as Hines Ward, Laveranues Coles, Chad Johnson, Plaxico Burress, and Donald Driver.

YEAR 2003

Running backs reasserted their dominance this season as twelve of the top sixteen fantasy point-getters were runners. Several new ones became fantasy forces, including Rudi Johnson, Domanick Davis, and Brian Westbrook.

YEAR 2004

Along with Manning and Culpepper pacing a monster quarterback season and the tight end position becoming greatly improved, this season marked the end of Marshall Faulk as an impact fantasy performer. Considered a late first-round, early second-round pick before the season, Faulk's rushing yards ended up going down a third straight season. He scored just four touchdowns, the lowest of his NFL career, which began in 1994. He enters the 2005 season a likely backup to Steven Jackson.

Even though many quarterbacks enjoyed fine seasons, this was a down year for wide receivers. The two best, Randy Moss and Terrell Owens, suffered injuries. But it wasn't just injuries. A trend in 2004 was for tight ends and number two-type wide receivers to have more passes thrown their way. A number of complementary wide receivers who opened the season as their team's second option had big seasons in 2004. Muhsin Muhammad, Javon Walker, Isaac Bruce, Drew Bennett, and Reggie Wayne all finished in the top ten in receiving yards. Each of those players, except Bruce, also scored at least 11 touchdowns. This showed that middle-to-late round wide receiver picks could turn out to be golden.

12. HANDICAPPING

GAMES AND TOTALS

You don't need to bet games to be successful in fantasy football. However, you do need to handicap the matchups and be aware of what over/under totals the linesmaker has set. This gives you a guide on how many points figure to be scored. Oddsmakers know what they're doing when they set the lines. Trust me—I worked for the best, Roxy Roxborough. The company Roxborough formed in the early 1980s, Las Vegas Sports Consultants, still makes the betting numbers for most of the sports books in Nevada.

Handicapping isn't nuclear physics—it's harder. Just kidding, of course. The fantasy football owner's goal is simply to put out the best fantasy football lineup each week. But that involves a lot of work, which handicapping is. Studying betting lines isn't just a gambling thing. It's an excellent source of information on who's going to win and by how much. Over/under totals at 45 points and higher are an indication there's going to be lots of scoring. Linesmakers usually set totals in the 37 to 44 point range. If the total is lower than that, don't count on many touchdowns. In 2004 there were only four totals below 33 points. There were 18 games that had over/unders above 50 points. All other games fell in the 34 to 49 point range.

Let's say the Rams are seven-point favorites against the 49ers with the total at 47. The oddsmaker is projecting the Rams to win 27-20. Another example is if the line on the Lions-Bears matchup is Bears minus 3 with an over/ under of 37. The oddsmaker is estimating the Bears to win 20-17. The linesmaker comes up with these figures by making power rankings. He takes into account statistics, home field, and injuries, while also factoring in a guess on which way the general public figures to bet. You don't have to do nearly that amount of work.

You're not going to pull your star players no matter what the matchup is. But handicapping comes in handy when deciding on the best kicker, defense, and wide receivers to use each week. It helps, too, in deciding what free agent choices you make for the week. Chances are when dipping into the free agent pool you're going to be looking at a lot of "C" and "D" players. So who they're playing against that week, and what their own situation is, makes all the difference. The trick is getting a "C" player the week he performs like a "B" player. To do that, though, you must be able to accurately analyze and project his matchup for the week. If a reserve running back is going against the league's worst run-defense and figures to get some carries, then he might be worth picking up for that week.

During bye weeks just about every owner is left scrambling for wide receivers. You're not going to find a top player like Joe Horn sitting in the free agent pool.

Chris Horn, yes. Joe Horn, no. But in Week 7 of the 2004 season I found Jerome Pathon available. He was the Saints' number three wideout behind Horn and Donte Stallworth. The Saints were playing the Raiders that week. From my handicapping, I knew the Raiders had trouble at the nickel and dime positions. So it was actually an advantage to take a team's number three receiver against them because their star cornerback, Charles Woodson, would be concentrating on the opponent's number one wideout. Pathon caught six passes for 79 yards that game. The following week the Saints were on a bye. I thanked Pathon and sent him packing back into the free agent pool. That was the most passes Pathon caught in a game all season. He was only valuable for that particular matchup.

So handicapping isn't just knowing numbers, but studying players. You really need to do both.

WEATHER AND FIELD CONDITIONS

Ever see a missed field goal at Miami's Pro Player Stadium, or quarterbacks having a poor performance at Giants Stadium?

Chances are the elements had something to do with that. The missed field goal in the Dolphins game probably occurred when the kicker had to kick in the infield dirt part of the stadium, while frequent strong winds can play havoc with quarterbacks in Giants and Jets games.

Pittsburgh's Heinz Field is another brutal place for kickers. Kris Brown made just eleven of twenty-one field goals there for the Steelers during his last seven games with Pittsburgh in 2001, while also missing three extra point kicks. No kicker has made a field goal longer than 48 yards at Heinz Field during the stadium's first four years. San Francisco is difficult, too. The 49ers have had four kickers the past three years going into 2005. Chicago isn't known as the Windy City because the Cubs win. Playing quarterback in Chicago is rough. The Bears have made twenty-six starting quarterback changes the last six years entering 2005. The Bears have had many great players in their illustrious history, but few outstanding quarterbacks. Of the twenty-six Bears enshrined in the Pro Football Hall of Fame, only two are quarterbacks, Sid Luckman and George Blanda.

Games played in rain and snow draw attention. They're fun to watch—if you're not there in person. It's because they are such a rarity. From 2001 to 2003, only six games were played in snow conditions. There's only been an average of two really heavy snow games a season the past four years. Bad weather doesn't factor in nearly as much anymore. It's not like the old days when Minnesota and Detroit didn't have domed stadiums. Pro football usually is played in excellent conditions, especially now that Philadelphia's Veterans Stadium is finally no longer around to end careers with its hard, unforgiving turf. Nearly half of the thirty-two teams play on artificial turf, with eight teams playing in a dome or retractable dome.

So don't downgrade a player if he happens to play in a cold weather site. If my drafting decision comes down to Jets quarterback Chad Pennington or a quarterback who is just a shade below Pennington in my ratings, I'm still taking Pennington. But if all things were equal, then

I would go with the other quarterback, just because of the tricky winds at Giants Stadium.

Rain and snow aren't nearly as bad as playing in a stiff wind or torrential rains. Those are the elements you need to be most aware of when setting your lineup. Snow by itself isn't necessarily a bad thing. Don't overreact to it if you have good players scheduled to play in that game. Wide receivers can have an edge in snow since they know where they're going, or at least some of them do.

The Raiders and Broncos combined for 49 points and nearly 600 yards passing in a late-November snowy game played at Denver during the 2004 season. Jerry Porter caught six passes for 135 yards and scored three touchdowns because All-Pro cornerback Champ Bailey couldn't stay with him in the snow. Porter made Champ look like a chump.

The Raiders treated a snow game like it should be treated—passing the ball. Many coaches, though, will become ultraconservative in bad weather games. That was the case in Week 15 of the 2004 season when the Chargers traveled to Cleveland to meet the Browns. The game was played in blowing snow with a subzero wind chill factor. Chargers Coach Marty Schottenheimer—and they don't get any more conservative than Marty—had quarterback Drew Brees throw just six times against a Browns defense that was allowing an average of 45.6 points their previous three games.

HANDICAPPING

Rain and Wind

You can't ignore weather. It can be a huge factor, ruining passing attacks and messing up kickers. Adverse weather can seriously affect the game and your fantasy numbers. Heavy rain and swirling winds are what you most need to pay attention to. There are top-notch weather sites on the Internet that provide not only instant updated information, but long-range forecasts. These sites need to be added to your bookmarks. I start checking on weather as early as Tuesday. You wouldn't want your quarterbacks or receivers in the Steelers-Dolphins game played September 26, 2004. A hurricane had just struck the South Florida area and the weather was still bad. The game was played in a downpour and footing was treacherous. The teams couldn't pass that night (not that A.J. Feeley could throw even in perfect conditions), and only 16 points were scored.

Cold Weather

The hurricane game was an obvious example of weather affecting play. Another was the Colts-Patriots playoff game from the 2004 season when record-setting Peyton Manning could only steer his offense to three points because of freezing temperatures, despite New England missing both its starting cornerbacks. Weather can equalize talent. It can make a mediocre, plodding runner look good, and slow down a dangerous sprinter. Some players aren't affected by cold and bad conditions. Brett Favre is 37-3 at home when the temperature is 34 degrees or below as he enters the 2005 season.

Be careful, though, when starting players from warm-weather cities and domed stadiums at cold-weather sites. I've never trusted the Dolphins in December road games, especially at New England where they were shut out in 2003 playing in a blizzard. Starting around mid-November bad weather can become a concern. You may have the best kicker, but if there are gusting winds, his coach probably won't let him attempt long field goals if kicking against the wind. This is why it can be useful to carry two kickers once November rolls around. This way you're covered, not only in case of injury, but weather-wise, too.

COACHES

Mark Twain once said, "There are three kinds of lies: Lies, damned lies, and statistics." To this fine list we add a fourth category of lies: Coaches' lies. Coaches may be forthcoming during preseason about injuries and player rotations, but once the regular season begins they are about as truthful as someone adding up his golf score or figuring out his income tax.

Coaches and Injuries

Some NFL coaches may be personable. Some may be brilliant. All seem hard-working, but none can be trusted. It's naïve to think otherwise. Sooner or later you'll get burned by their soft-pedaling an injury or listing someone as questionable when that player has about as much chance of playing as Jimmy Hoffa has of turning up.

HANDICAPPING

Those who had Ravens tight end Todd Heap or Patriots wide receiver Deion Branch in 2004 know what I speak of. Branch suffered what turned out to be a fairly serious knee injury early in the season. He missed seven straight games starting in Week 4. Patriots Coach Bill Belichick, the most notorious when it comes to releasing truthful injury reports, said Branch was doubtful to play in Week 4. Actually, Branch had no chance of playing. Then Belichick kept listing Branch as questionable up until Branch finally returned in Week 11. Heap suffered a twisted right ankle against the Steelers in Week 2. Ravens Coach Brian Billick kept fantasy owners twisting in the wind by never revealing the full extent of the injury. By the time Heap finally played again in Week 13, many of his fantasy owners had already cut him out of frustration.

Mike Tice burned me bad during Week 7 of the 2004 season. I started a gimpy Randy Moss that week despite a hamstring injury. I played Moss because he's a superstar and Tice said Moss would play. Yeah, Moss played all right. He was a decoy the first two plays, then exited and sat out the rest of the game. I ended up losing my head-to-head match by four points that week.

You can say, "Why gamble? Don't take the chance on Moss being unavailable. Get someone in who can get you some points." Ordinarily I'd agree with that thinking. But there are a handful of superstars, who if the coaches says they are going to play, you have to go with them. Moss certainly is one of those players.

Titans Coach Jeff Fisher and Steve McNair are another disgusting injury act. It's always a game-time decision with these two about McNair's playing status, and the final decision always comes after the deadline time for your lineup to be in. Guess wrong just once on McNair playing or not and you're left without a quarterback for the week. Good luck winning your match without one. McNair's toughness actually works against him here. If McNair were more brittle, then you know he wouldn't be in the lineup.

Of course there's Mike "Pinocchio" Shanahan and his weekly juggling of running backs. Who's the starter this week—Quentin Griffin, Reuben Droughns, Tatum Bell, Garrison Hearst, Floyd Little, Floyd the Barber? When it comes to being straightforward, Shanahan makes Bill Clinton look like George Washington.

The worst con of 2004, though, was Eagles Coach Andy Reid holding out a healthy Brian Westbrook and pulling Donovan McNabb after just three passes in Week 16. Yes, Reid was entitled to do this, since the Eagles had already clinched home-field advantage throughout the playoffs and the game was meaningless. But what ticked so many fantasy players off was that Reid never said he would do this.

He gave the impression Westbrook would play, and left people guessing how long McNabb would be in. Since this was a meaningless game for Philly, what would have been the big deal if Reid said he was going to hold Westbrook out and limit McNabb? It just happens Week 16 is the championship week in many fantasy leagues. Those who had Westbrook or McNabb most likely had their title hopes crushed.

Coaches and Passing

While coaches make good secret agents when it comes to guarding injuries, they are easier to read when it comes to their offensive philosophies. There are those who prefer a wide open style. Mike Martz, Dennis Green, and Dick Vermeil fit this category. Quarterbacks playing under them have an excellent opportunity to put up huge numbers, although Green sheds starting quarterbacks faster than Paris Hilton sheds clothes. A few coaches will even keep their quarterback passing late in the game when their team has already locked up the win. Martz is known for that. Steve Spurrier wasn't above doing that either. Spurrier was the rare NFL coach who had the potential for actually running up a score. Unfortunately for him, his only opportunities for doing that during his brief NFL career came during preseason.

You can often do well if you can fit the player into the right system. Kurt Warner was transformed from Arena Football League/grocery clerk into NFL superstar when he got a chance to operate Martz's high-powered Rams offense in 1999. It was the perfect system for Warner, a pocket passer with a strong arm. He put up 41 touchdowns and more than 4,300 yards throwing in '99. Marshall Faulk and Priest Holmes became fantasy superstars as the featured backs in Dick Vermeil's offensive system, which he ran when he coached the Rams and later the Chiefs.

Certain old-school coaches like Bill Parcells and Tom Coughlin are never going to deviate too much from trying to run the ball a lot. That's their comfort zone. Conversely, there are Bill Walsh-disciple coaches like

Mike Holmgren, who favor a passing-type of West Coast offense. The Raiders have a long-standing tradition of throwing long passes.

Sometimes that can lead to a mediocre receiver making a fantasy dent. Speedster James Jett, for instance, averaged 843 yards and scored a combined 18 touchdowns in 1997 and 1998. Back in the mid '90s, Falcons Coach June Jones installed a run-and-shoot offense. Jeff George was the lucky recipient of this ultra-aggressive passing game. George threw for an NFL-best 4,143 yards in 1995. Unfortunately, that offense hasn't been in vogue the past ten years. Neither has George's sideline rants.

Coaches and Running

Many coaches have defensive backgrounds. This usually makes them extra cautious on offense. They play the field position battle. This is good for their running back and kicker, but not their quarterback and wide receivers. In this group are Jack Del Rio, Marty Schottenheimer, John Fox, and Dom Capers. These guys can get so conservative with their play-calling they seem to the right of Jesse Helms.

Some coaches are flexible enough to adjust to their existing talent. Brian Billick was the Vikings' offensive coordinator when they set the NFL record for most points in a season with 556 during 1998. Billick loved to pass, but he has been forced by his talent at hand to be a conservative, run-oriented coach with the Ravens because he's never had a top-flight quarterback.

Mike Mularkey was an innovative offensive coordinator with the Steelers before he became the Bills' head coach in 2004. He made a wise decision midway through the season to ride Willis McGahee rather than go with any kind of sophisticated passing attack with an immobile and aging Drew Bledsoe. The Packers' Mike Sherman featured Ahman Green as his main offensive weapon in 2003, but switched back to Brett Favre and an emphasis on the passing game because of the weak secondaries on his 2004 schedule and an early season-ending injury to center Mike Flanagan, an excellent run blocker.

Monitor New Coaches

It's important not just to look at the head coach, but also at his offensive coordinator and quarterback coach as well. Teams will change their style of attack. Often this occurs when a new head coach or coordinator is brought in. Pay close attention to this and monitor things. A systems switch can work for or against a player. When Atlanta changed to a West Coast offense in 2004 under first-year head coach Jim Mora Jr., I immediately downgraded Michael Vick. He's best in a free-wheeling style, not a tightly restricted passing game. Vick put up 902 rushing yards, but was twenty-sixth in passing yards. He threw for only 14 touchdowns.

DEALING WITH BYE WEEKS

Don't forget bye weeks when making free agent pickups. You know when teams are going to be idle, so plan a week or two in advance of them.

OPPOSING DEFENSES

No matter how outstanding a defense is, even if it's a defense as dominant as the 1985 Chicago Bears, don't bench your best players if they're going against it. Your decisions may come down to who to start at quarterback, if you have similar caliber quarterbacks, or what third wide receiver to put in. If your lineup is solid all the way through, your only choice may be who to use at the flex position.

You don't want to be intimidated by an opponent's defense or let that defense cause you to overmanage your lineup. Some weeks it's best just to play your regular starters and not worry about the teams they are going up against. Still, you need to be aware of what defense you're going against, and see if there are moves you can make that would increase the chances of you winning.

Consider if the defense is home or away. Road defenses aren't as strong in most cases. This is one of the main criteria I use when selecting a fill-in defense when my number one defense has its bye week. There aren't going to be any really strong defenses left in the free agent pool, so at least try to get one playing at home the week your starting defense is idle.

Don't just gloat looking at how well your skill position players are performing. Study defensive statistics. A team could be really good against the run, but weak against the pass. Check the team's schedule. Have they piled up impressive statistics against easy opponents, or are their stats skewed downward because their competition has been so strong?

All things being equal, it makes sense to play matchups. If your opponent's defense has a porous secondary, and you're undecided on which quarterback to play, that should factor strongly in your decision. If the defense you're playing against happens to use a 3-4 alignment geared to stop the run, think about going with a wide receiver instead of running back at your flex spot.

Look deeper than just the numbers. Through the first six weeks of the 2004 season, for example, the Falcons ranked number one against the run while playing mainly inferior offenses. In Week 7, though, the Falcons were blasted 56-10 by the Chiefs. The Chiefs ran for 271 yards and scored an NFL-record eight touchdowns on the ground.

Current form, though, is usually important. How has a defense been playing lately? A cluster injury problem in the defensive line, linebacker, or secondary can greatly reduce the effectiveness of a defense. The Seahawks surrendered just 13 points in winning their first three games of the 2004 season. But then they started having multiple injuries at linebacker and their defense fell apart.

With free agency and injuries being so common, reputations come and go faster. In the early 2000s, you respected a number of defenses like the Ravens, Buccaneers, and Titans, especially when they were at home. But a lot of luster came off those defenses in 2004. So in the rapidly changing world of the NFL, don't get locked into old perceptions. Change with the times.

The same holds true for individual defensive players. There are no dominant cornerbacks anymore since the NFL decided prior to the 2004 season to emphasize defensive pass interference by tightening the chuck rule, where defenders can't touch a receiver after five yards. Full proof of this came during Week 12 when the Broncos' Champ Bailey, regarded as the league's finest cornerback, covered the Raiders' Jerry Porter.

Some Porter owners decided not to play him that week because of that matchup. They also were frustrated that Porter had tallied just one touchdown up to that point. But Bailey had trouble handling Porter, who caught six passes for 135 yards and scored three touchdowns. Two of Porter's scores came when directly matched up against Bailey. Just three weeks later, the Chiefs' Eddie Kennison beat Bailey for two touchdowns, while catching seven passes for 101 yards.

This isn't to knock Bailey but merely to point out some big-name players might not be as dominant as their reputation leads you to believe. Brian Urlacher, for instance, was named by *The Sporting News* as the most overrated defensive player of 2004.

INJURIES

Injuries are a huge part of football. But let's be honest. Violence is part of the allure of football, and injuries are a byproduct of that. Yes, a major injury to a superstar on your team can be devastating. Know that going in so you can be prepared to deal with it if it happens. You're not playing fantasy croquet. This is football. Things could be worse. It could be you on those crutches, or with the broken collarbone.

HANDICAPPING

This is where a strong bench comes into play. Always be on the lookout to improve your team, even if it means shoring up your strongest position. Fortunately, most injuries aren't the season-ending kind. Familiarize yourself with terms like ACL, MCL, stinger, Grade I concussion, turf toe, and charley horse.

Injury reports come out every week in the NFL. There are four classifications: A player listed as probable has a 75 percent chance of playing. Someone listed as questionable is 50-50. A player only has a 25 percent chance of seeing action if listed as doubtful, while out means the player won't play. Coaches are subject to huge fines by the league if they list someone as out and the player ends up playing anyway. This rarely occurs. However, coaches are known to fudge on their weekly injury reports.

A lot of coaches don't like to reveal the true status of a player. This keeps the other team—and fantasy football owners—guessing whether or not the player will play. The questionable status is the most dreaded. One of the worst phrases a fantasy football owner can hear is, "Game time decision." For a while I thought Steve McNair's full name was Steve McNair Game Time Decision.

Out is obviously a no-brainer as far as your strategy. Doubtful status is too risky. A player listed as probable is worth the gamble, unless you have a backup of equal value, or a slightly lesser player who happens to be in a more favorable matchup that week than your injured starter. Coaches aren't going to help you with these decisions. The Russian KGB has nothing on NFL coaches when it comes to putting out disinformation.

But there are ways of increasing your chances of making the right decision on when to use or not use a player listed on the injury report. It helps to learn something about the most common football injuries, and the severity level of them.

Knee injuries happen a lot. You're talking ligament and cartilage damage here. Ligament is the more severe injury of the two. The worst is a torn ACL, which stands for anterior cruciate ligament. Your player isn't coming back quickly if he sustains that injury. There's also medial collateral ligament, which isn't as nasty as ACL.

There are different levels of concussions and sprained ankles. If a player suffers a Grade I concussion, he probably can play the following week. His status is iffy if he has a Grade II concussion. Grade III is the most severe. That one can keep a player out a while. The ankle sprain you have to look out for is a high ankle sprain. That can keep a player out anywhere from three to eight weeks.

Charley horses are just a fancy name for leg cramps. Usually they're nothing to worry about. But a pulled or torn hamstring can bother a player a long time, as Randy Moss owners found out the hard way during the 2004 season. Moss never seemed to be his dominating self after suffering a partially torn hamstring the sixth week of the season.

Stingers and turf toe sound funny, but they're nothing to laugh at. A stinger is a painful injury where nerves in the neck get stretched. Turf toe is an injury to the big toe, which can linger and eventually keep a player from suiting up, as Chris Brown owners sadly discovered in 2004.

Plantar Fasciitis can be a debilitating injury, too. That injury involves the arch of the foot and restricts a player's cutting ability.

It helps to have an idea of a player's pain tolerance. Just about everyone in the NFL is tough, but some players have a history of playing with so-called minor bumps and bruises. Curtis Martin has been amazingly durable. Chris Brown hasn't. Brett Favre never gets sidelined. Chad Pennington seems fragile. Daunte Culpepper and Peyton Manning appear indestructible. Michael Vick is vulnerable with his reckless style.

Unless there's a huge drop-off in talent, I don't like to take chances with injuries when deciding on a starter for that week. I've been burned too many times with game-time decisions on players listed as questionable. It happened in 2004 to owners who had Fred Taylor, Stephen Davis, Duce Staley, Chris Brown, Corey Dillon, and Steve McNair. These guys were all game-time decisions who ended up missing at least one week when many of their owners had them in the lineup.

You're almost always okay using players listed as probable. Sometimes you can find out Friday or Saturday that those guys will play despite their injury designation. A red flag goes up, though, if they get downgraded to questionable, don't practice all week, or suddenly back track, saying they aren't as confident they can play as they were earlier in the week. That was the tip-off that Fred Taylor wouldn't be able to go during the second-to-last week of the 2004 season. The result was the Jaguars were shut out 21-0 by the Texans, and fantasy football owners who played Taylor during that crucial Sunday probably lost their playoff game.

Some online leagues allow you to change your lineup right until kickoff. If your league has that kind of setup you can be a little more daring with injured players since you can switch at the last minute. Just don't be late like I was trying to get William Green out of my lineup after finding out five minutes before kickoff he had been kicked out against the Steelers for getting into a pre-game fight with Joey Porter. As soon as I heard that I rushed to the computer, but by the time it booted up and got the league Web site on the screen, the game had started. Moral of that story is leave your computer running on Sunday, at least until the games kick off.

Injury Effects on Other Players

Injuries can affect your players even if they aren't the ones hurt. A starting quarterback being knocked out can severely impact wide receivers. You don't want to have any wide receivers in your lineup if the quarterback throwing to them has a last name of Detmer or McCown. A quarterback injury can also hurt the statistics of the featured back. The Bears' Thomas Jones went three months without rushing for 100 yards after quarterback Rex Grossman suffered a season-ending knee injury at the end of his Week 3 game against the Vikings during the 2004 season. Before Grossman went down, Jones had rushed for 152 yards and 110 yards, respectively.

Your running back's statistics can be negatively affected, too, if he relies on the lead blocking of a fullback and that fullback gets hurt. An injury to an offensive tackle may result in fewer passes being thrown to your tight end because he might have to help out blocking more. Of course, practically any offensive line injury isn't good for your skill position players. There aren't too many teams in the NFL with very good depth in the offensive line.

So take at least a moment and examine the potential ramifications of an injury, even if it's not to your player.

MENTAL ASPECTS

Every year some fantasy football owner gets hit with a key injury to his team. It's inevitable. It was Terrell Davis and Jamal Anderson who suffered serious injuries in 1999. Joey Galloway went down in 2000. The following season it was Edgerrin James who had his season end prematurely. It was the same with Kurt Warner in 2002. Michael Vick missed a large portion of the 2003 season. Priest Holmes missed half the season in 2004. I feel your pain. Believe me I do. I had four of my first six picks in my 2004 draft league miss significant time with injuries. Consider yourself lucky if you lose only one player.

Unlike real football players, we don't have to deal with the physical aches and pains, just the mental. But that's enough. Try to keep a positive attitude. Okay, the nightmare becomes reality and you lose your franchise running back. Great, now you have a built-in excuse why you didn't make the playoffs.

Seriously, try to stay calm. Perhaps you have first crack at the free agency pool and waiver wire. So you can get some of those numbers back, especially if the team's backup runner is available for you to pick up.

Remember Dominic Rhodes rushed for 1,104 yards and scored nine touchdowns in ten games for the Colts in 2001 after replacing an injured James. Marc Bulger threw for 1,826 yards and accounted for 15 touchdowns when he replaced an injured Warner during the final seven games of the 2002 season. Larry Johnson gained 541 yards and scored 11 touchdowns during the Chiefs' final six games of 2004 with Holmes sitting out. You never know. All is not necessarily lost. You must keep battling. Maybe there are some trades avenues worth exploring. Keep all options open.

Try to maintain your equilibrium. It's important not to get too high or too low. Never allow yourself to get over-confident, especially in head-to-head matchup leagues. I've seen terrible teams, some even starting players on their bye week, knock off previously unbeaten teams. Chances are when rookie Clarence Moore caught two touchdown passes for the Ravens on the road against the Jets in Week 10 of the 2004 season, some fantasy owner had Moore in his lineup.

Limit the Number of Teams You Own

Part of the mental challenge is staying on top of your team or teams. I find managing three teams to be enough. That's my limit. Any more and you start losing track of which players are on which teams. You don't want to end up rooting against some of your players because you're going against too many of those same players in other leagues. I remember getting an e-mail response back from one owner in an online league regarding a trade offer I had made him. This was three weeks ago. Sorry for the late response, the owner wrote, but I just got around to studying your trade offer because I'm in eighteen different leagues. What's the point of owning every player in the league? That's like playing roulette and betting every number.

Keep the Game in Perspective

For the vast majority, fantasy football is all about having fun. It's not a profession; it's a hobby. It's entertainment. Keep it in perspective. Don't let yourself get loaded down with too much information where you're ordering a Kerry Collins instead of a Tom Collins to drink at your draft.

You don't want to get your head so clogged up where you can't tell the difference between Chester Taylor, Travis Taylor, and James Taylor (Chester's the running back, Travis is a wide receiver, and James is a singer who is worth about as much as Travis when it comes to fantasy football).

Dealing with the Family

The toughest mental aspect can be dealing with family. Let's face it—not all family members are going to be as interested as you are when it comes to fantasy football. You're not going to find too many grandmothers asking if Tim Rattay threw any touchdown passes. It's great if somehow you can get them hooked. I've seen father and son teams, even a few dad and daughter teams and husband and wife teams. If you can somehow interest your lady (or man) in fantasy football, then more power to you. That would be a remarkable achievement. Most women can't comprehend why men are so passionate about their sports, especially football.

To keep harmony, you may have to pick your spots. My wife, for instance, isn't a football fan. She wouldn't know Donovan McNabb from Donovan the '60s folk-pop singer. My deal with her is that she takes the baby during the day on Sunday, so I can watch and root in peace without any diaper changes.

In return, I have to give up either the Sunday night game or Monday night game. If you have a similar arrangement, then don't pick a Monday night game to miss when there are two bad defenses playing. I made that error during Week 14 of the 2004 season when the Chiefs and Titans met. There were 12 touchdowns, 670 passing yards, 309 rushing yards, and Drew Bennett caught 12 passes for 233 yards and scored three touchdowns in the game. That was the game I gave up in order to accompany her shopping. Luckily I found a nearby electronics store in the mall, and was able to catch some of the big plays while hiding behind the baby stroller.

It is worth keeping good relations. Just remember football games come and go. Families are forever.

13. ETIQUETTE

There's no need to read Miss Manners or Amy Vanderbilt, but etiquette is appreciated in fantasy football. Your fellow owners don't care if you gulp your food or guzzle your beer during the draft, but they may get offended if you make them a horrific trade offer.

Before mindlessly sending a trade offer out, study your opponent's roster. You might desperately want one of his players, but who would he realistically want in return? Be objective. Be fair. It's a source of pride that owners in my face-to-face league have told me they appreciate the fair offers I make. They know when they see an e-mail coming from me with "Trade Offer" in the subject field it's not spam. It's something to be taken seriously.

If you're trying to trade for a superstar, chances are you're going to have to give one back or at least deal two solid players in return. Don't lowball someone. I needed running back help going into Week 8 of the 2004 season. I traded for Thomas Jones, giving up Donovan McNabb in return. I thought it only fair to offer McNabb since Jones was having a big season at the time. Naturally Jones carried the ball one time for me before getting hurt and missing the next two games.

You don't want to be wasting someone's time. There's nothing more disappointing than getting a trade offer and finding out it's a proposal of the Dolphins kicker and Donte Stallworth for Randy Moss. That was an offer I actually received for Moss in 2004 while he was recovering from his hamstring injury. It's tempting to send an e-mail back ripping that owner for making such an insulting offer. One owner I know makes it a point to send out an even worse trade offer if he gets a trade proposal he believes is unfair. But it is best not to get caught up in all that. Instead, cool off and send a simple, "No thank you."

Never try to trade an injured player or someone likely to be suspended unless you make sure the other owner knows about it. It's one thing to be cutthroat, it's another to be dishonest. Full disclosure is in order. You can't always assume the other owner knows as much as you. In a sports writer's basketball fantasy league I was in, a fellow owner once received a call in the press box while covering a game. It was from another league owner trying to trade him a player.

Luckily for the working sports writer, he was on deadline. So he said he would get back to the other owner. When he returned to the newspaper, he found out the player offered to him suffered a knee injury that night and was out for the season. Turns out the shady owner who made the offer had been watching the game and was hoping to make a quick deal before anyone found out. That's sleazy. It's not worth it. Be upfront about injuries. You don't have to be so honest as to say, yeah, I think this player could be benched in a couple of weeks when so-and-so returns from an injury. But never hide injuries. It is bad karma and it ruins your reputation. Seasons come and go, but the reputation and trust you build stays.

One time I received an e-mail from an owner offering me a decent player for a much lesser player. Only one problem. The guy he was offering had just been suspended for the season. I knew about it because I happened to be online at the time. The story had just broken and wasn't more than twenty minutes old. I wasn't interested in making a trade with that particular owner ever again. That owner also happened to be the commissioner. I left his league after the season.

It's not only fair, but can be advantageous, to let each league member know if you're seriously shopping a superstar. That way no one feels left out, or didn't have an opportunity to get the player. It can prevent bruised feelings. Plus, you never know what kind of offer you might get. It's disconcerting to discover after dealing a player that another owner would have given you more.

Just alert the league, though, when you're looking to trade a superstar or player at a specialized position where there's a scarcity. Don't bother people by sending out a league-wide e-mail or post a bulletin board message saying, "Jay Fiedler available," or "Willing to trade Quincy Morgan." You'll look stupid. Keep it to players with value.

Keep trade negotiations friendly. Treat e-mail messages the same as if you were talking face to face or on the phone. Owners are very protective of their players. They can get offended when you rip their players. Use a positive approach when dealing. Respect the fact that there are differences of opinion. Fantasy football would be very boring if everyone held the same views. If some owner keeps taking Ron Dayne every year, then God bless him.

The same applies after a trade is made. Don't brag or cut down the other owner if you make a good trade. If you were left out of a trade, or thought a trade was totally one-sided, resist the temptation to vent. Don't rip owners on the message board. It might feel good at the time, but it's not worth it. I did it when I first started playing fantasy sports, and it has taken me years to live down the perception that I'm a hothead. It doesn't accomplish anything. The owners you blast feel insulted and probably won't ever deal with you. The rest of the league might get a chuckle and agree with what you wrote, but they're not going to do anything.

Treat your league's message board and posting forum very carefully. Some guys like to talk trash. Let them. I've rarely seen a trash talker win a league. Usually the ones who talk the biggest have the least self-confidence. You have more important things to do, like handicapping and studying players, than waste time putting up cocky messages that you have no way of knowing you can back up while alienating fellow owners.

ETIQUETTE

Look, I know a fantasy football draft isn't exactly the same as a solemn, dignified religious ceremony. But a few tips on draft etiquette can't hurt. Here are ten suggestions:

1. Resist the temptation to scream when the person right before you picks the player you've been coveting. It's not only ill-mannered, but now you've tipped your hand. This makes it harder to trade for that player because the other owner is going to drive the price up, remembering how much you desired that player. If it's any consolation, having a player snatched right before your pick has happened to all of us. It's to the point where you almost expect it.

2. Don't rip someone else's pick. We're talking ego and pride here. No one likes to be criticized, even if you think it is totally justified. One year an owner took Moe Williams—in the third round. Eyebrows certainly were raised, but no one said anything until one owner blurted out, "Was that Moe Howard (of Three Stooges fame)?" To which another owner said, "Moe Howard would have been a better pick." To which a third owner said, "So are you going to take Curly or Shemp next?" A good laugh was heard around the room, except from the embarrassed Moe Williams owner.

3. Be ready when your turn comes. Hopefully your league has a time limit. There's nothing worse than waiting around forever while some unprepared owner frantically pages through magazine after magazine shouting out players who have already been picked.

4. Keep track of what players get chosen. It's embarrassing to you and highly annoying to everyone else if you call out a name that already went. One owner took his full minute and then proudly announced he was taking Anthony Thomas. This was in the fifteenth round. Thomas, who at the time was the Bears' featured runner, had been taken twelve rounds earlier. From then on the sheepish owner kept asking if so-and-so had been picked yet. This also was very irritating.

5. Don't get so drunk that people have a hard time understanding the name you're calling out. You don't want to look at your team roster the next day and find out you have Kevin Faulk instead of Marshall Faulk.

6. Try not to get too sarcastic. This closely ties in with not ripping somebody's pick. A few years ago Jeff George was a hot fantasy commodity. After he was selected, an owner deadpanned, "I'd rather have Boy George." Another owner followed with, "Yeah, Boy George is tougher." Most owners are good-natured. But it doesn't hurt to know the makeup of your league. How serious do guys take things? Are they okay being kidded?

7. Feel free to pay sincere compliments. If someone makes an astute pick or gets value late on a good player everybody seemed to forget about, don't be afraid to say, "Nice pick," or "Well done."

8. Refrain from making innocuous comments on obvious things, like saying, "Great pick" when Priest Holmes goes number one.

9. Not that you would, but don't ever ask to see another owner's cheat sheets or player notes. Try to sit a respectable distance apart. That way everyone has privacy. Fantasy football is about fun, but competitive fun. I'm probably way too much of a hardliner, but I don't even like an owner asking to borrow my pen. I do bring extra pens just in case, though.

10. No table talk. The worst thing is hearing some yokel ask before his pick if so-and-so has been taken yet. One idiot owner even said during a 2004 draft, "I can't believe Javon Walker hasn't been picked yet." Well guess what? Walker went on the very next pick. Walker ended up finishing the season third in receiving yardage and fifth in touchdowns among wide receivers.

14. PLAYOFFS

The regular portion of your fantasy football schedule has ended and you've made it to the Promised Land, otherwise known as the playoffs. Now what? If you're lucky, nothing. Hopefully there's no need to switch dance partners. Stick with the studs and starters who got you this far. It's rare, however, to have that luxury. You almost always have to do at least some minor tweaking with your lineup.

The playoff structure varies depending on the league, but often consists of two weeks involving the top four teams. You have the semifinals and the following week the championship game. Some leagues use just a one-week championship format, perhaps pitting the overall points-leader against the team that had the best won-lost mark, or have two division champions meeting to decide the overall winner. There are leagues that stretch their playoffs into three or even four weeks. Some leagues also have a consolation playoff where all the teams who didn't qualify are thrown together. That's when your pride is really tested, because there's often no monetary or tangible incentive.

If you're realistically in playoff contention, then think down the road. Start preparing for the playoffs several weeks in advance. Are there any potential players in the free agent pool who might have a chance of putting up good fantasy stats during Weeks 13, 14, 15, 16, or 17 when fantasy playoffs take place?

One sharp owner plucked the Cowboys' Julius Jones out of free agency in Week 8 during Jones's rookie season of 2004. Jones had been out since the second week with an injured shoulder and wasn't scheduled to return until around Week 13. The owner stashed Jones on his roster, hoping he had found a stud running back at a cheap price. Sure enough, Jones came back earlier than expected, returning to full-time duty in Week 11. In the final six weeks, Jones averaged 120 yards rushing, caught 15 passes and scored seven touchdowns.

If I know my league playoffs occur in Weeks 15 and 16, I'm looking hard at the schedule and the free agency pool to see if there might be any defenses or kickers in great situations those weeks. I start doing this several weeks in advance. It doesn't pay to pick up a defense for Week 16 in Week 8 because so much can change. Things become more clear once teams start wrapping up playoff berths and home-field advantage for the playoffs. The Eagles, for instance, clinched home-field advantage for the playoffs in Week 15 in 2004.

This rendered their final two games meaningless. Immediately you should start thinking about who the Eagles' next two opponents are. It's a little different facing Koy Detmer, Jeff Blake, and Eric McCoo than Donovan

McNabb and Brian Westbrook. The Eagles concluded their regular season against the Bengals, so picking up and starting the Bengals defense for Week 17 would be a consideration if your league had its championship game that final week.

Sure enough, the Eagles held out all their big guns and the Bengals handily won, 38-10. The Bengals defense ran back an interception for a touchdown, picked up five turnovers from the Eagles scrubs, and recorded three sacks.

The flip side is those playoff owners who had McNabb and Westbrook got shafted if their playoffs were held in Week 16 and 17. McNabb threw three passes those final two weeks and Westbrook never even played. It was a similar situation with Michael Vick when the Falcons clinched the number two playoff seeding early. Vick was held out of Week 16 and threw just seven passes in Week 17. Peyton Manning made just a token appearance, throwing two passes in the Colts' meaningless regular season finale in 2004 against the Broncos.

Sure, you would like to stick with your stars through the playoffs, but sometimes the timing and situation put you at too much of a disadvantage. Teams clinching play-off spots early and holding out their star players until the playoffs is the bane of fantasy football. It's frustrating for fantasy owners, but it's hard to blame the coach. He's earned the right to rest his star and not take any injury chances. It's a well-deserved reward. That's why many fantasy leagues end their playoffs before Week 17, the final Sunday.

However, wacky spots often happen in Weeks 15 and 16, too. It's late in December by then, so weather can be a factor. Take that into consideration in making out your playoff lineup. Those playoff owners who had a quarterback choice and went with Drew Brees during Week 15 of the 2004 season received a rude shock. The Chargers were playing the lowly Browns. But the game was in Cleveland where there was heavy snow. So Brees passed just six times for 85 yards and one touchdown. The Chargers' game plan was so conservative, you wonder if Rush Limbaugh devised it.

Other bizarre things can happen, too, this late in the season. Teams no longer in playoff contention may quit playing hard, or insert inexperienced players into their lineup to build for next season. This could lead to favorable fantasy matchups if you have a player going against such a club.

Stay active. Keep making moves even if you have already clinched your playoff position. This is football, so the injury factor is always prevalent. Terrell Owens suffered a severe ankle injury in Week 15 of the 2004 season during an Eagles victory against the Cowboys. If you had Owens and your championship playoff game was the following week, you were left scrambling unless your bench was stocked with good backup wide receiver choices.

Injuries happen often, both early and late. If one of your starters gets hurt and is questionable during your playoffs, don't chance it. There is no way you can take zero points at any position during your playoffs. I cost myself a league championship in 1995 by starting Mark

Brunell as my quarterback in Week 16. Brunell wasn't quite 100 percent. He was listed as probable on the injury report, so I thought it was safe to go with him. He didn't play that week. That's always stuck with me. It's been ten years since that happened, and I've never started someone in the playoffs if there was even the slightest doubt he might not play.

You have to be prepared. Think contingency. That means making sure you have enough quality backups to combat the unexpected, like injury, suspension, or whatever reason. It's easy to get caught in the euphoria and rush of making the playoffs. One or two of your players gets hot, the rest are steady, and you ride right into the postseason. But keep your equilibrium. The week of your playoffs you might find some of your players on the road in bad weather conditions going against a tough defense.

There's no second-guess about playing your franchise running back and best wide receiver. Decisions enter in other areas like your number three receiver, flex, defense, and kicker. I recall Antowain Smith of the Bills rushing for 147 yards and scoring three touchdowns against the Seahawks in the team's final regular season game of the 2000 season. Smith had rushed for under 300 yards up to that point in the season, but the Seahawks ranked third from the bottom in rush defense.

Here's another example, this one from Week 16 of the 2001 season. Let's say you have a decent kicker, but in your playoff finals your kicker is on the road against a solid defense. It's a grass field and the forecast calls for gusting, swirling winds. This would be a time to play matchup and see if there is a kicker in free agency in a much better situation. That was the case here with the Redskins' Brett Conway.

Normally he's too inconsistent to be a fantasy starter but in this spot he was kicking inside a dome against the Saints, who ranked among the five worst defenses in allowing points. The Saints were free-falling, having failed to once again make the playoffs. Sure enough, the Redskins put up 40 points against them. Conway was four for four in field goals with a long of 53 yards and also kicked four extra points.

So you never know. It doesn't hurt to have plenty of options. Stay active in free agency and carefully scan the waiver wire. There just might be a borderline starter available who has a highly favorable matchup in Week 15, 16, or 17. You've come this far. It would be a shame to get caught short with everything on the line.

END OF SEASON BANQUET

Having an end of season banquet is a nice way to celebrate, or commiserate, the end of a season with your fellow owners. It can stabilize and improve league morale to have an end of season get-together. The first-place winner can treat or buy the drinks. Or everyone can just pick up their own tab. It's not about the money. It's about the camaraderie and fostering league fellowship. Our yearly destination is Hooters. The food isn't for epicurean tastes, but the beer is cold and the scenery is to our liking.

Having an end of season banquet is also an easy and personal way to distribute checks to those who finished in the money. Some leagues even present a trophy to the winner. That's certainly better for the winner than getting a Yoo-hoo shower.

The setting is a lot calmer at end of the season banquets than when everyone is together at the draft. People aren't nervous or tight-lipped, anxiously awaiting the beginning of the draft. They're not loaded down with reams of notes and notebooks. It's a stress-free, informal atmosphere. It's a great chance to communicate, cement friendships, and just banter with people who share a similar interest.

This is an opportunity to review your league's rules, while eliciting feedback on whether anyone wants to make any changes. We've come up with several refinements in our league structure from ideas tossed around during our annual banquet.

It's a chance for the winner to brag, and for the rest to vent about their rotten luck, injuries, and bad beats. Where else can a fantasy football owner find sympathy and understanding for such things as officials not awarding Travis Henry a sure touchdown, a kicker missing an extra point, Brian Westbrook being held out of a meaningless game with your season on the line, David Carr doing nothing after you just traded your top running back for him, and Randy Moss suffering his first injury the year you finally get him in the draft? It almost becomes a contest for each owner to top the other one with tales of woe.

Your wife, girlfriend, mother, and child aren't going to understand these laments. Let's face it—most likely your wife is only too glad that damn fantasy football season is finally finished. Only your fellow league owners can relate to your trials and tribulations. They alone know the depths of your anguish. They are kindred spirits. So an end of season banquet can prove therapeutic. No need to consult a shrink. Are shrinks even qualified to understand what fantasy football participants go through?

If not, this could open up a whole new branch of medicine—psychologists specializing in tormented fantasy football owners. Perhaps it's time to put out a shingle and hang an Edvard Munch painting on the wall.

Best of all, at the banquet you can start firming up plans, and even set a date for next season's draft. Now that alone is worth an end of season gathering.

IF I WERE KING

Actually, I'd rather be commissioner of the NFL than king of the world. There's not too much difference between the two.

But if I were commissioner, just for one day, I would hand down a number of edicts.

1. NFL head coaches must be considerate of fantasy football players. That means no fudging on injury reports. They must be completely honest. If they know a player isn't going to suit up, no listing him as questionable or as a game-

time decision. If a coach is caught lying, he has to miss the game. That means Bill Belichick won't get to see many games.

2. No kneel downs are allowed. Every play has to be run. If protecting a lead late in the game, the quarterback has to at least try to cross the line of scrimmage. Running up the score no longer should be frowned on, but instead encouraged. Coaches need to think about fantasy owners rather than hurting the feelings of their opposing coach. It's time to get priorities in order.

3. No running back by committee is allowed. Not only must each team designate their starting running back, but they must prove it by giving that back a minimum of 15 carries. Got that Mike Shanahan and Steve Mariucci? If their main back falls short of the required number of carries, they must start Mike Cloud the following week.

4. All places of employment must provide ample company time each week for their employees to research and prepare their starting fantasy lineups.

5. No skill position player can sit out games or play less than two quarters, no matter how early his team clinches home-field advantage for the playoffs. Do you hear that Andy Reid? If a coach violates this policy, the backups have to see the same amount of action in the playoffs. Yeah, the star player could risk injury, but we must be fair to fantasy owners. Their interests should always come first.

6. All games should be televised and available for everyone to watch no matter where they might live. Also, Mike Patrick, Joe Theismann, and Paul Maguire shall be forbidden from ever broadcasting another game and are financially responsible for every eardrum they've shattered.

7. There will be a new annual award given in conjunction with the Most Valuable Player trophy. This award honors the player who had the most value to fantasy football owners. So in 2004 it wouldn't have been Peyton Manning, since he was picked in the first or second round. The Most Valuable Player trophy of 2004 would go to an unsung player who ended up producing unexpected monster numbers, like Muhsin Muhammad, Jake Delhomme, or Drew Bennett.

8. Any money won via an official fantasy football contest becomes tax free. Why should the
   government get a share of money you earned
   through your fantasy football acumen, not to
   mention your blood, sweat, and tears? The IRS
   should appreciate what it takes to win a fantasy
   football contest.

15. THE LAST WORD

I used to be able to do Rotisserie baseball and fantasy basketball, too, along with football. I gave up baseball a few years ago. It's called getting a life. The realization hit me when I kept an out-of-town visiting girlfriend waiting for forty-five minutes while I pored over baseball box scores.

When I finally got up from the computer, her packed bags were by the door and a taxi had just pulled into my driveway. I couldn't convince her to stay. She wasn't impressed when I told her my pitcher's ERA and ratio had gone down for the week, and I had picked up four stolen bases on the day.

Now I'm down to just one online league in basketball besides my football commitments. The problem is if I give up fantasy basketball, I'll never be able to watch an NBA game again. How can you possibly root for some of these punks and guys whose names you can't pronounce if you don't have a fantasy involvement?

Compete, root, have fun. That's really what fantasy football is all about. I try not to lose sight of that. I love football, and fantasy football enhances that enjoyment. Hopefully it does for you, too.

Best of luck and may the REAL best team win!

THE CHAMPIONSHIP SERIES
POWERFUL BOOKS YOU MUST HAVE

CHAMPIONSHIP OMAHA (Omaha High-Low, Pot-limit Omaha, Limit High Omaha) by Tom McEvoy & T.J. Cloutier. Clearly-written strategies and powerful advice from Cloutier and McEvoy who have won four World Series of Poker titles in Omaha tournaments. Powerful advice shows you how to win at low-limit and high-stakes games, how to play against loose and tight opponents, and the differing strategies for rebuy and freezeout tournaments. Learn the best starting hands, when slowplaying a big hand is dangerous, what danglers are and why winners don't play them, why pot-limit Omaha is the only poker game where you sometimes fold the nuts on the flop and are correct in doing so and overall, and how you can win a lot of money at Omaha! 296 pages, photos, illustrations, New Edition! $29.95!

CHAMPIONSHIP STUD (Seven-Card Stud, Stud 8/or Better and Razz) by Dr. Max Stern, Linda Johnson, and Tom McEvoy. The authors, who have earned millions of dollars in major tournaments and cash games, eight World Series of Poker bracelets and hundreds of other titles in competition against the best players in the world show you the winning strategies for medium-limit side games as well as poker tournaments and a general tournament strategy that is applicable to any form of poker. Includes give-and-take conversations between the authors to give you more than one point of view on how to play poker. 200 pages, hand pictorials, photos. $39.95.

CHAMPIONSHIP HOLD'EM by Tom McEvoy & T.J. Cloutier. Hard-hitting hold'em the way it's played today in both limit cash games and tournaments. Get killer advice on how to win more money in rammin'-jammin' games, kill-pot, jackpot, shorthanded, and other types of cash games. You'll learn the thinking process before the flop, on the flop, on the turn, and at the river with specific suggestions for what to do when good or bad things happen plus 20 illustrated hands with play-by-play analyses. Specific advice for rocks in tight games, weaklings in loose games, experts in solid games, how hand values change in jackpot games, when you should fold, check, raise, reraise, check-raise, slowplay, bluff, and tournament strategies for small buy-in, big buy-in, rebuy, incremental add-on, satellite and big-field major tournaments. Wow! Easy-to-read and conversational, if you want to become a lifelong winner at limit hold'em, you need this book! 388 Pages, Illustrated, Photos. $39.95. Now only $29.95!

CHAMPIONSHIP NO-LIMIT & POT-LIMIT HOLD'EM by T.J. Cloutier & Tom McEvoy. New Cardoza Edition! The definitive guide to winning at two of the world's most exciting poker games! Written by eight time World Champion players T.J. Cloutier (1998 and 2002 Player of the Year) and Tom McEvoy (the foremost author on tournament strategy) who have won millions of dollars each playing no-limit and pot-limit hold'em in cash games and major tournaments around the world. You'll get all the answers here—no holds barred—to your most important questions: How do you get inside your opponents' heads and learn how to beat them at their own game? How can you tell how much to bet, raise, and reraise in no-limit hold'em? When can you bluff? How do you set up your opponents in pot-limit hold'em so you can win a monster pot? What are the best strategies for winning no-limit and pot-limit tournaments, satellites, and supersatellites? You get rock-solid and inspired advice from two of the most recognizable figures in poker—advice that you can bank on. If you want to become a winning player, and a champion, you must have this book. 304 pages, paperback, illustrations, photos. $29.95

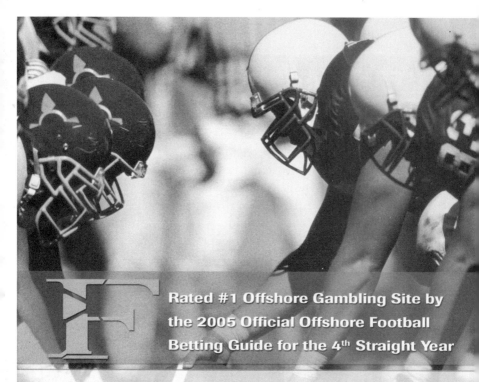